Lecture Notes in Energy 6

For further volumes:
http://www.springer.com/series/8874

Francesco Gullì

Pollution Under Environmental Regulation in Energy Markets

Springer

Francesco Gullì
Via della Torre 14
Milan, Italy

ISSN 2195-1284 ISSN 2195-1292 (electronic)
ISBN 978-1-4471-4726-8 ISBN 978-1-4471-4727-5 (eBook)
DOI 10.1007/978-1-4471-4727-5
Springer London Heidelberg New York Dordrecht

Library of Congress Control Number: 2012954488

Printed on acid-free paper

Springer is part of Springer Science+Business Media (www.springer.com)

Preface

This volume comprises the results of the author's extensive research conducted over the last three years at the Department of Policy Analysis and Public Management of Bocconi University and at the European University Institute of Florence (Florence School of Regulation).

The research activity has been funded by the Italian Ministry of Education, University and Research (Miur) in the context of the "Environmental Policy under Imperfect Competition in Energy Markets" research project, carried out with the collaboration of the Bocconi University Center for Research on Regional Economics, Transport and Tourism (CERTeT).

The results of this project have been presented and discussed in several international conferences and seminars. The author would like to express his gratitude to the participants of these seminars for their remarks and suggestions, which helped greatly in improving both the content and the results of this research work. However, the content of this book reflects only the views of the author.

Finally, special thanks to Annamaria Pastore for her patience and for her expert editing and proofreading of the volume.

Milan, Italy Francesco Gullì

Contents

Chapter 1
Introduction and Summary

Abstract This chapter introduces the topic of this book and explains why it is important to study how imperfect competition can affect the ability of environmental regulation to reduce pollution and/or to minimize the cost of meeting environmental targets. After a short review of the relevant literature, this chapter illustrates the content of each part of the volume describing the main findings and the policy implications. In this respect, it should be interpreted as the executive summary of the overall analysis.

1 The Topic

For many years, the International community has been committed to reduce or at least contain anthropogenic environmental pollution. In this field one of the main objectives is the GHG (Greenhouse Gases) emissions reduction. This commitment has triggered numerous worldwide initiatives.

In 1997, the Kyoto Protocol was signed. In 2005, this protocol was ratified by a quorum of countries whose GHG emissions represented 55 % of emissions worldwide. In the 2008 "EU climate and energy package," the European Union set the goal of reducing GHG emissions by 20 % by 2020. In many developing and developed countries, GHG emissions containment policies have been implemented or are being implemented.

These policies are usually twofold: (1) targeted interventions, aimed at promoting specific low carbon and carbon-free technological solutions (e.g., policies aimed at supporting renewable energy sources); and (2) general policies aimed at promoting pollution reduction, regardless of how this reduction is met.

In this last category two main environmental policy tools are included, namely: environmental taxes and the tradable emission permits (upon which Emissions Trading Schemes—ETS are based).

In the case of taxation, policymakers establish a monetary value per each pollutant unit emitted (tax rate). This represents the pollution price and can be

F. Gullì, *Pollution Under Environmental Regulation in Energy Markets*,
Lecture Notes in Energy 6, DOI 10.1007/978-1-4471-4727-5_1,

applied, instead of directly on emissions (emissions tax), indirectly on the inputs (input tax) whose use is primarily responsible for pollution (e.g., the fuel used for producing electricity or heat). The tax could then induce pollution reduction if it promotes the adoption of abatement technologies (including the shift to less pollutant input and processes) and if it raises the output price (which influences the demand). Therefore, in the tax case the independent variable (exogenous) is the pollution price and the dependent one (endogenous) is the emission reduction.

In the case of tradable emissions permits, the independent variable is the target (emissions reduction) and the dependent one is the pollution price. Policymakers establish the reduction emission target and allocate to polluters a number of permits consistent with this target (a quantity of permits adequately lower than their past or expected inertial emissions). At the end of the compliance period, each polluter should surrender a number of permits equal to its emissions for that period. To reach this objective, the polluter has two options (or a combination of them): emission abatement or/and to buy permits from other companies. This mechanism gives rise to the market for permits. The corresponding price can be interpreted as pollution price. If companies consider it cost-effective, they could lower their emissions more than they need and sell excess allowances. In principle, companies able to reduce most emissions are those having the lowest abatement cost. Therefore, the overall cost of meeting the environmental target should be minimized.

However, regardless if we consider taxes or emission permits, the environmental policy requires the choice of an emission reduction target. This is a direct choice in the case of emission trading permits and represents an indirect one in the case of taxation (once the curve of the marginal abatement cost is estimated, policymakers choose the level of tax that could ensure compliance with the set environmental target).

To this purpose, economic theory suggests that the optimal level of reduction happens when the marginal abatement cost is equal to the marginal damage cost of polluting (marginal abatement benefit). However, it is difficult to apply this principle for the following reasons. Firstly, the curves of both marginal abatement costs and benefits are highly uncertain. Secondly, environmental regulation impacts on a heterogeneous group of countries and individuals with different interests and needs. Therefore, its implementation requires reaching a consensus among all parties involved. This applies mostly when the environmental impact is global and the choice of the environmental target requires, such as in the case of global warming, an equitable commitment in reducing emissions among various countries and regions with different levels of richness, pollution and different developmental needs and perspectives. However, the need of large consensus arises even within one single country or an aggregation of countries whereby various groups of interests attempt to influence the environmental policy design.

As a consequence, target definition is also a political choice reflecting stakeholders' consensus (firms, consumers, institutions).

This does not imply that the target is set without taking into account scientific and technical issues. In fact, the chosen target, and the distribution of the effort to meet it, will instead result in a compromise among the scientific instances and the pressures exerted by different countries and regions and, within those, the pressure exerted by the various interest groups.

However, political mediation is not entirely abstract. The latter happens (or it is hoped it would happen) through an accurate evaluation of the environmental policy impact at global, country, regional, and market levels.

To evaluate this impact, policymakers resort to micro and macro simulation models able to produce a series of important outputs: environmental performance, namely the ability to induce an emission reduction in the short and long-run; the impact on the gross domestic product (GDP); the environmental regulation costs and their distribution amongst firms and consumers; the impact on the competitiveness of the different industrial sectors; etc.

By comparing various results and conducting a sensitivity analysis, policymakers choose a target and its distribution able to guarantee a wide consensus of all parties involved. At the same time this choice must be consistent, for as much as possible, with scientific and technical issues (e.g., in the case of global warming, consistent with the objective of stabilizing GHG concentration in the atmosphere). Therefore, economic simulation models have a great responsibility in addressing environmental policy choices. In fact, they help to calibrate reduction targets and also to verify the performance of environmental tools.

These models are generally based on a series of hypotheses concerning both the structure and operation of energy markets which are largely responsible of GHG emissions.

A fundamental assumption of these models is that energy markets are fully competitive or behave as such. In the first case, the fully competitive outcome is simulated. In the latter case, the models claim to internalize market power simply by applying a mark-up to competitive prices without taking into account how the strategic behavior of firms can change their production share and how this, in turn, can impact on prices. This essentially means that changes in prices, in production and in emissions are the same occurring in the absolute fully competitive outcome, under the usual conditions of the demand function.[1]

As, often, this does not reflect the reality of most cases, simulations may provide a biased representation of environmental policy impact leading to underestimate or overestimate its performance. This prompts to check what could happen when the assumption of full competition is removed. In fact, imperfect competition, by means of its impact on prices, combined with the strategic use of supply capacity, may largely affect the performance of environmental policy as long as it has impact on costs, on prices and on the share of production of the different polluting technologies and, consequently, on emissions.

[1] With linear downward sloping demand (variable price elasticity) the outcome is the same, however it is different if iso-elastic demand is assumed.

2 The Literature

Just a few authors focused on how imperfect competition can affect the performance of environmental regulation.[2] Unfortunately, their contributions provide controversial results.

On the one hand, focusing on Cournot competition, Levin (1985) states that "If output and pollutant levels are positively correlated, then sharp concavity in demand will result in increased pollution".[3] Similarly Requate (2005) demonstrates that "if firms are sufficiently asymmetric, namely whose cost functions are sufficiently different, then it is possible that, for particular tax-rate intervals, aggregate emissions are increasing".[4] However, for the last effect to arise, asymmetry of firms does not suffice. The inverse demand function must show an extreme curvature,[5] i.e., it must be either sufficiently convex or sufficiently concave.

On the other hand, Canton et al. (2008) analyze environmental taxation in vertical Cournot oligopolies and discover that an increase in the tax rate always induces a reduction in the output produced in a downstream (polluting) market and higher levels of environmental goods purchased in the upstream market. At the same time, Sugeta and Matsumoto (2007) state that "... an increase in pollution taxes always reduces the total pollution emissions." This result would arise regardless of the kind of taxation, that is whether on input (input taxes) or on emissions (emission taxes).

In line with the existing literature, the approach used in this work is theoretical. Nonetheless, it is not generic (namely based on the analysis of generic production activities) but it specifically simulates the operation of energy markets with their crucial specificities. In this respect, we hope that this approach could provide a

---

[2] It is to be noted that, apart from those described herein, there are other groups of studies examining the possible adverse effect of environmental regulation. Among them we should mention the contributions by the authors studying the so-called "green paradox" (Sinn 2012; van der Ploeg and Withagen 2010). However, this book does not take into consideration these contributions explicitly because they do not refer specifically to the link between environmental regulation and market structure (imperfect competition).

[3] Levin considers Cournot competition. In his model the firms' cost functions depend on output only. The author does not consider abatement technologies. For another interesting contribution using the Cournot framework see Requate (1993).

[4] Following Requate (2005) the intuition is that if the marginal cost differential between the firms is different from the difference in emission coefficients, taxation changes the cost structure between the firms. This can not only lead to a situation where one firm gains, whereas the other firm suffers from a tax increase, but can also cause aggregate pollution to rise. Requate achieves this result by using a cost function depending on output and emissions that is by accounting for abatement. However, he also underlines that if the tax rate is set sufficiently high, so that each firm's output goes down, then aggregate emissions also have to go down, compared to the laissez-faire level.

[5] Chernyavs'ka and Gullì (2009) find that this condition is not necessary for increasing pollution. However, these authors focus on the particular case of the electricity market and carry out a short-run analysis (without abatement technologies).

further contribution to clarifying the controversial framework arising from the current literature.

To understand the relevance of this contribution, it is necessary to make the following premises:

1. We concentrate just on environmental performance. We do not attempt to measure the overall change in social welfare. This measurement may be misleading since it requires estimating the economic value of environmental damage which is largely uncertain. The main aim is instead to simply identify the mechanisms through which imperfect competition can interact with environmental regulation.
2. The focus is not on the comparison of the different market structures in absolute terms, namely the difference in emissions at any one time. Instead, we are simply interested in the change of this variable over time. As explained later, this is important in order to calibrate the public action and to estimate its economic effects.
3. In both cases, taxes and permits, the environmental performance is evaluated by comparing full to imperfect competition, and in particular by checking the probability of increasing pollution not only in the long-run but also in the short-run under imperfect competition. In fact, increased pollution in the short-run can undermine meeting long-run targets, in the case of taxation, and can lead to an increase in the cost of meeting the long-run target, such as the case of ETS.
4. Finally, to simulate market power, a dominant firm facing a competitive fringe model is adopted.[6] This model is used in the literature concerning environmental policy under imperfect competition and it is well suited to simulate the structural features of several energy markets.

3 Content and Results

This volume comprises three chapters, in addition to the introduction. These chapters are independently structured and refer to a specific energy sector (or combination of energy sectors). Each chapter is a stand alone, therefore the reader will find all needed information and explanations about the specific application in the relative chapter without the need of searching them elsewhere in the book. Obviously this might imply some overlaps in the overall text.

[6] This model is used in the literature on the environmental policy under imperfect competition, see See Conrad and Wang (1993), Bonacina and Gullì (2007), Chernyavs'ka and Gullì (2008) and Gullì (2008). On the methodological side, the attraction of this characterization is that it avoids the implausible extreme of perfect competition and pure monopoly, at the same time escaping the difficulties of characterizing an oligopolistic equilibrium. In particular, this model allows us to overcome the problem of possible inexistent equilibria in pure strategy.

Chapter 2 focuses on the analysis of the residential sector (essentially space heating). The case of space heating is particularly interesting as it implies inter-technology competition under which hybrid regulation is possible. Hybrid regulation happens when different environmental regulations are applied to different supply technologies (delivering the input for useful heat generation) which coexist in the same market (e.g., tradable permits to electricity supply for space heating and energy or emissions taxes to district heating or natural gas supply and vice versa). This analysis explores how hybrid regulation can affect the performance of environmental policy, namely its ability to reduce pollution, and/or its ability to minimize the cost of meeting environmental targets, when markets are imperfectly competitive. Different kinds of environmental taxation (on consumers and on producers, on inputs or on emissions) and, under ETS, different methods of allowances allocation (auctioning, free allocation) are taken into consideration. Regulatory pressure, possibly exerted by regulation and sector-specific authorities, is not considered. Finally, numerical simulations are carried out in order to check the theoretical results.

Chapter 3 concentrates on electricity sectors (wholesale spot power markets). This case is also topical as it illustrates what might happen when markets are organized in the form of multi-period and multi-unit price auctions and firms' behavior is affected by the regulatory pressure exerted by competition and sector-specific public authorities.

Finally, Chap. 4 is a sort of extension of the previous chapters. It studies the performance of environmental policies under imperfect competition in vertical related energy markets, namely the natural gas market (input) and the electricity market (output). This time both the case of regulatory pressure and the case without regulatory pressure are considered in order to compare the corresponding results. In addition, two technological scenarios are investigated: (1) Scenario 1 (highly polluting supply) in which power generation is based on more polluting technologies; (2) Scenario 2 (cleaner supply) in which power generation is based on cleaner technologies.

The three chapters provide a wide range of results which can be summarized by the following key findings:

1. In line with part of the current literature, the theoretical analysis of residential sectors proves that environmental regulation may increase pollution at least in principle. However, this analysis also demonstrates that this result does not require either extreme curvature (sharp concavity) of the inverse demand function or sufficiently large asymmetry of firms. Furthermore, some apparently counterintuitive results arise. Firstly, under taxation the perverse effect might be more likely if taxes are charged to producers rather than to consumers, whereas common sense would suggest that taxation should always work better when regulation is able to stimulate emissions abatement and not only the decrease in demand through the impact on prices. Secondly, free allocation of emissions allowances (combined with pricing regulation) drastically reduces the probability of increasing pollution. Finally, hybrid regulation seems to play a

significant role in affecting the probability that environmental policy could lead to a perverse effect (or could avoid it). Nevertheless, this role is ambiguous. Compared to symmetric regulation, hybrid regulation can lessen or amplify the probability of increasing pollution depending on several factors. Numerical simulations only partially confirm the theoretical results. Increasing pollution is unlikely or very unlikely in several situations where it is theoretically admissible. In addition, the simulations highlight that the perverse effect of environmental policy is admissible in several situations where the dominant technology is more polluting than the fringe technology. This result might confirm the risk of trade-off between environmental regulation and policies aimed at supporting cleaner technologies. In fact, when polarized configurations are due to energy policies promoting the deployment of cleaner technologies (fringe technology), environmental regulation can lead to a dual effect, at least in principle. It might increase the risk that the dominant firm prefers to undercut the cleaner technology rather than to accommodate its production, and, at the same time, leading to increasing rather than decreasing pollution. However, the numerical simulations also show that in these situations the probability of increasing pollution, although admissible, is relatively low. As a consequence the risk of the above-mentioned dual effect, in real terms, is modest. Furthermore the analysis shows that the perverse effect of environmental policy arises only for particular pollution price intervals, namely if the pollution price is sufficiently low, lower than that value involving a switch in cost-efficiency between the dominant firm and the fringe. If the pollution price is above this "switching" value, pollution almost never increases.

2. Under imperfect competition in electricity sectors, the main finding of the analysis shows that, in line with some contributions of the current literature, imperfect competition may increase pollution (at least in principle and in the short-run) in specific time-periods, namely in specific hours of the relevant supply period (day or year). However, this may happen only under specific and unlikely conditions. In addition, if we look at the entire demand cycle, it emerges that absolute pollution increase is virtually impossible.
3. When both the output (electricity) market and the input (natural gas) markets are imperfectly competitive, the analysis shows that the pollution cost of the gas-fired plants does not depend on their own emission rate but on that of their main alternative. Then imperfect competition may lessen the ability of environmental policy to reduce pollution (in the short-run). In principle this would occur regardless of the power supply scenario (Scenario 1 or Scenario 2) and regardless of the kind of environmental regulation (whether based on pollution taxes or on emissions trading and, in the latter case, regardless of the type of allowance allocation, whether based on auctioning or benchmarking). However in Scenario 2 it can only occur if pollution prices are relatively low. In both scenarios, increasing pollution in the short-run seems to be more likely when firms can maximize profits rather than under regulatory pressure, unless firms pursue long-term profit targets and environmental regulation is based on ETS with benchmarking. The analysis also highlights that an absolute increase in

pollution, at least in the short-run, cannot be excluded not only in specific time-periods (specific groups of hours of electricity demand) but also considering the entire power demand cycle. Nevertheless, it is important to point out that this is unlikely to occur even when firms pursue a long-term profit target and regulation is based on ETS and benchmarking of emissions allowances. Therefore, pollution increase is virtually excluded.

In conclusion, and as mentioned earlier, the current literature on environmental policy under imperfect competition provides controversial results. In relying on generic analytical models, some contributions demonstrate that environmental regulation could never lead to increased pollution, whereas others state that the perverse effect of environmental policy is admissible.

The analysis carried in this volume seems to suggest avoidance of excessive generalization since the outcome crucially depends on market specificities.

When firms face a single demand curve (space heating), the theoretical analysis confirms that increasing pollution is widely admissible in principle, in line with the above-mentioned second group of contributions, but it does not require large (environmental) asymmetry of firms. However, when real market and technology conditions are accounted for (by means of specific numerical simulations), increasing pollution can be excluded or is very unlikely in many situations where it is theoretically admissible.

Furthermore the probability of increasing pollution depends on the kind of environmental regulation but this relationship, in turn, depends on market organizational and regulatory specificities. For instance, ETS with free allocation of emissions allowances (combined with pricing regulation) sharply reduces the probability of increasing pollution in the market for space heating. At the same time, as explained above, free allocation of emissions allowances may sharply increase this probability in electricity market (at least in specific time-periods and in the short-run).

If vertical related markets are considered, imperfect competition in both markets can significantly affect the probability of increasing pollution. This probability depends on how environmental regulation modifies the cost structure between technologies. This, in turn, depends on the main alternative technology to the input delivered under conditions of imperfect competition. For instance, when the dominant technology is more polluting than the fringe one, if the alternative technology is highly polluting, imperfect competition in both related markets (input and output) reduces the cost asymmetry between technologies. This makes the perverse effect of environmental policy more likely. If the alternative technology is low polluting (transition toward cleaner markets), the cost asymmetry between technologies goes up and increasing pollution becomes less likely.

When we go beyond the context whereby firms face a single demand curve (the case of space heating), the outcome significantly changes. In electricity markets, where demand varies cyclically over time and firms compete within multi-period price auctions (wholesale spot markets), increasing pollution (in the short-run) becomes virtually impossible or very unlikely even in principle, looking at the entire demand cycle.

However the analysis also highlights that, although increasing pollution is in this case virtually excluded or very unlikely, imperfect competition can significantly affect the performance of environmental policy, lessening or amplifying its ability to reduce pollution and/or to minimize the cost of meeting environmental targets, compared to full competition. Even in this case, the outcome depends on the specificities of energy markets and cannot be generalized. Nevertheless, the probability that imperfect competition could lessen the performance of environmental policy seems to be higher if pollution prices are relatively low. Then two policy implications arise.

Firstly, it is crucial to take into account the specificities of energy markets in order to explain how environmental regulation interacts with market structures. Therefore if the models used to estimate performances and costs of environmental policies ignore the full role of imperfect competition (the impact on prices combined with the strategic use of supply capacity) and the specificities of energy markets, this may induce incorrect estimations of the cost of public action and/or (depending on the kind of environmental tool used) might lead to incorrect policy calibrations, depending on how the policy targets are set.

Secondly, if environmental policies are quite modest, imperfect competition in energy markets significantly amplifies the risk of overestimating the performance of public action.

Finally, it is worth pointing out that this volume is based on a series of basic assumptions about the operation and the structure of energy markets. In order to avoid overlaps, these assumptions are discussed only in the last chapter of this book (Chap. 4).

References

Bonacina M, Gullì F (2007) Electricity pricing under "carbon emission trading": a dominant firm with competitive fringe model. Energy Policy 35:4200–4220

Canton J, Saubeyran A, Stahn H (2008) Environmental taxation and vertical Cournot oligopolies: how eco-industries matter. Environ Resour Econ 40:369–382

Chernyavs'ka L, Gullì F (2008) Marginal CO_2 cost pass-through under imperfect competition. Ecol Econ 68:408–421

Chernyavs'ka L, Gullì F (2009) Environmental taxation within electricity auctions with dominant firm. International Energy Workshop (IEW) proceeding 2009, Venice

Conrad K, Wang J (1993) The effect of emission taxes and abatement subsides on market structure. Int J Ind Organ 11:499–518

Gullì F (2008) Modeling the short-run impact of carbon emissions trading on the electricity sector. In: Gullì F (ed) Markets for carbon and power pricing in Europe: theoretical issues and empirical analyses. Edward Elgar, Aldershot, UK and Brookfield, WI

Levin D (1985) Taxation within Cournot oligopoly. J Public Econ 27:281–290

Requate T (1993) Pollution control in a Cournot duopoly via taxes or permits. J Econ 58:255–291

Requate T (2005) Environmental policy under imperfect competition – a survey. CAU, Economics Working Papers, no 2005–12
Sinn H (2012) The green paradox. The MIT Press, Cambridge, MA
Sugeta H, Matsumoto S (2007) Upstream and downstream pollution taxations in vertically related markets with imperfect competition. Environ Resour Econ 38:407–432
Van der Ploeg F, Withagen C (2010) Is there really a green paradox? CESifo Working Paper no. 2963

Chapter 2
Pollution Under Hybrid Environmental Regulation: The Case of Space Heating

Abstract Economic literature on environmental policy under imperfect competition provides controversial results. Some contributions find that under specific conditions environmental policy can increase emissions. Others find that environmental policy never increases emissions. However, these contributions are based on symmetric environmental regulation. The same environmental tool is applied to all firms and/or consumers belonging to a specific industrial or service sector. This chapter aims at studying how these results are affected by hybrid regulation when different environmental tools are applied to technologies coexisting in the same sector. This situation is well-suited to describe the structural and technological features of space heating in residential sectors. Looking at polarized market configurations (a dominant firm facing a fringe of producers), the analysis shows that increasing pollution is widely admissible in principle and does not require large environmental asymmetry of firms. However when the real conditions of markets and technologies are accounted for (by means of specific numerical simulations), the probability of increasing pollution seems to be very low in most situations where it is theoretically admissible. The results about the impact of hybrid regulation are ambiguous. Compared to symmetric regulation, hybrid regulation plays a significant role in affecting the probability of increasing pollution. However, this role cannot be generalized.

1 Introduction

Space heating is among the major causes of environmental pollution. It represents one of the most interesting cases of analysis of the relationship between environmental regulation and market structure.

Heat for space heating can be produced by means of several technological solutions using different inputs: light fuel oil or natural gas fired combustion boilers; electric heat pumps; centralized production of hot water transported over relatively long distances by means of pipelines (district heating); etc.

F. Gullì, *Pollution Under Environmental Regulation in Energy Markets*,
Lecture Notes in Energy 6, DOI 10.1007/978-1-4471-4727-5_2,

Different environmental regulation can be applied to the different inputs for useful heat generation (and consequently to the different kinds of useful heat supply): tradable permits (with different types of allowances allocation) or environmental taxes (taxes on producers or taxes on consumers, emissions or input taxes). This implies that hybrid regulation is possible. In fact, since various kinds of heat supply may coexist, various combinations of environmental regulation may indeed coexist for the same final service (useful heat for space heating). For example, when useful heat is produced by natural gas boilers, the most likely regulation is based on input taxes on consumers. If useful heat is delivered by electric heat pumps the most likely regulation is ETS with auctioning or emission taxes on producers. If heat supply is based on district heating, environmental regulation may be based on ETS with free allocation of emissions allowances. Consequently, different kinds of regulation can coexist in the same market (hybrid regulation).

Then the question is: How does hybrid regulation affect the performance of environmental policy and, namely, the probability of increasing pollution? This chapter aims at answering this question.

In several countries, the technological structure of space heating is highly polarized. Generally, a specific technological solution covers the most part of consumption, whereby the other kinds of supply play a residual role (fringe supply).

In turn, input (for useful heat generation) markets may be characterized by quite different structures. Some of them may be close to the conditions of full competition whereas others are highly concentrated and, consequently, characterized by significant market power. Finally, in other input markets prices may be regulated.

In many European countries the leading technology is the gas-fired boiler facing electric heat pumps and/or district heating which play the role of fringe technologies. In other countries, the dominant energy supply technology is district heating or direct and indirect electricity technologies.

A typical situation of polarized market is when the dominant technology is operated by a dominant firm and a large number of price taker firms operates the fringe technology. Consequently, these markets can be adequately simulated by using a dominant firm with fringe model.

In this model, the leader maximizes its profit on residual demand. This implies that the production by the price taker firms belonging to the fringe is partially or totally accommodated depending on cost and demand shape curves. If cost curves are constant over a sufficiently large supply interval the dominant firm practically faces two choices: (1) maximizing its production by setting prices just below the price which would make the end user indifferent when choosing between its own technology and the fringe's technology (the indifference price); (2) setting prices above this price, accommodating the fringe's maximum production.

Given firms' capacities, this choice depends on two factors: (1) the residual monopoly price and (2) the cost structure of the technologies operated by either the dominant firm or the fringe.

Since environmental regulation can modify these two factors, it is in principle able to induce the dominant firm to change its choice when moving from the previous situation to that after the implementation of environmental regulation.

In this chapter, dedicated to space heating, we aim at checking whether and under which conditions this might happen and subsequently how it might undermine the performance of environmental policy, leading to increasing rather than decreasing pollution.

The theoretical literature has devoted great effort to studying environmental policy in presence of imperfect competition. As pointed out in the introduction of this book, the results of the existing literature are controversial. Some authors highlight that increasing pollution is possible under specific conditions in terms of supply and demand (Levin 1985; Requate 2005). Others demonstrate that environmental policy never increases pollution (Canton et al. 2008; Sugeta and Matsumoto 2007).

In line with this framework, this analysis concentrates on pollution taxes and emissions trading and does not engage in describing optimal level of the control policy. It focuses solely on comparative static effects. In fact, given the huge uncertainty about environmental damages,[1] searching for the optimal level of control policies might be less useful than exploring the effects of different levels of pollution prices (tax rates or carbon prices), if we mainly look at the policy implications of the analysis.

Two kinds of environmental regulation are investigated: taxation (on producers or on consumers) and emissions trading (with auctioning or free allocation of emissions allowances). Symmetric regulation arises when the same tool of environmental policy (e.g. only taxes on consumers or only ETS with auctioning) is applied to the different technology cycles. Hybrid regulation occurs when different tools are applied to different technologies.

In line with some contributions of the existing theoretical literature, the analysis confirms that the perverse effect of environmental regulation is widely admissible[2] and does not require large environmental (environmental) asymmetry of firms. However, increasing pollution might be less likely (1) when input taxes are applied to the dominant firm's consumers and (2) especially when environmental regulation is based on ETS with free allocation of emissions allowances combined with regulation of the fringe's prices. Finally, it emerges that hybrid regulation can play a significant role in affecting the probability that environmental regulation could imply a perverse effect. Nevertheless, this role is ambiguous. Compared to symmetric regulation, hybrid regulation can either increase or decrease the probability of increasing emissions depending on several factors.

This chapter is structured as follows. Section 2 presents the assumptions of the model. Section 3 focuses on how the environmental regulation can impact on pollution under imperfect competition. Section 4 carries out numerical simulations. Section 5 concludes.

---

[1] We mainly refer to the marginal cost of carbon dioxide emissions.

[2] For the specific case of the electricity markets, see also Gullì (2008).

2 Assumptions

Useful heat is produced in the consumption stage. Its inverse demand, $p(Q)$, depends on the aggregate output Q only and is twice differentiable with $-\infty < \partial p/\partial Q < 0$ for all Q. Firms belonging to the same sector deliver homogenous inputs for useful heat generation. For the sake of simplicity (and without loss of generality), the energy conversion efficiency, namely the ratio between the useful heat and the input, is normalized to one. As a consequence, the input demand and the demand for useful heat coincide (unless taxes on consumers are applied, as it will be explained later).

The pollutant is emitted in the production or in the consumption process and pollution is proportional to output.

Environmental regulation in input markets is based on pollution taxes (on producers or on consumers) or on emissions trading (ETS). Taxation is proportional to emissions and charged to the producers (emissions taxes) or to the consumers (to the input used to produce useful heat).

The pollution price, τ, is the charge per unit of pollutant emitted, namely the tax rate under taxation and the price of the tradable permits under emissions trading. The emission rate, $r > 0$, is the emission per unit of output.

The technologies are represented by their cost functions. We assume linear technologies whose cost per unit of output, q, is $c \geq 0$.

Firms have abatement technologies. Therefore the emission rate depends on τ and it is decreasing and convex, i.e., $\partial r(\tau)/\partial \tau < 0$, $\partial^2 r(\tau)/\partial \tau^2 > 0$ with $r(\tau) > 0$ for all τ. Total emissions are given by the emission rate multiplied by the output, $r \cdot q$, and consequently the total "pollution cost" is equal to the emissions multiplied by the pollution price, that is $r \cdot q \cdot \tau$. Following the literature on this topic (Requate 2005; Sugeta and Matsumoto 2007), the cost functions already incorporate the abatement opportunities. Pollution can be substituted for by using more of other abating inputs which in turn involve higher costs, that is $\partial c/\partial r < 0$. Furthermore, we assume that $\partial^2 c/\partial r^2 > 0$.

Under taxation, taxes will be charged to producers or to consumers. In the latter case, it is reasonable to assume that policymakers set the tax rate by adopting a reference (constant) emission rate. For instance it can be equal to the emission rate before taxation, $r(\tau) = r(0)$. Consequently, with taxes on consumers either the emission rate or the unit production cost does not depend on the tax rate, that is $r(\tau) = r(0)$ and $c(\tau) = c(0)$, $\forall \tau$.

Under ETS, permits are auctioned or allocated free of charge. Given these assumptions, the total cost function (conventional cost plus "pollution cost") for the technology cycle i will be

$$C_i(q_i, r_i, \tau) = c_i q_i + \tau\, r_i q_i - \tau\, \Gamma \tag{2.1}$$

where Γ is the amount of allowances allocated free of charge. This amount is calculated by setting a reference emission rate, r_{bn_i}, and a reference production level, $\bar{q}_i$. Then $\Gamma = r_{bn_i}\bar{q}_i$ and the average production cost will be

$$AC_i(q_i, r_i, \tau) = c_i + \tau\, r_i - \tau\, r_{bn_i}\gamma \tag{2.2}$$

where $\gamma = \bar{q}_i/q_i$ and $r_{bni} \in\,]0, r_i[$. The public authority chooses $\bar{q}_i$ on the basis of the historic production level (typical grandfathering) or on the basis of the expected (inertial) future production level. Obviously, $\bar{q}_i = 0$ under taxation and under the ETS with auctioning.

By differentiating (2.1) with respect to r_i, we get one of the first-order conditions for total cost minimization

$$\tau = -\frac{\partial c_i}{\partial r_i} \tag{2.3}$$

Therefore, given τ, a firm with inefficient abatement technology (higher $\left|\frac{\partial c_i}{\partial r_i}\right|$) chooses an abatement level lower than that chosen by a firm with efficient abatement technology.

Two groups of technological solutions are available, $i = a, b$, with $c_a < c_b$, $r_b < r_a$ or $r_b > r_a$ and $\left|\frac{\partial c_a}{\partial r_a}\right| < \left|\frac{\partial c_b}{\partial r_b}\right|$ or $\left|\frac{\partial c_a}{\partial r_a}\right| > \left|\frac{\partial c_b}{\partial r_b}\right|$ respectively. Furthermore, when $r_b < r_a$ there exists a pollution price, the "switching price," $\tau_s = (c_b - c_a)/(r_a - r_b)$, such that the marginal cost of the technology a, MC_a, is equal to that of the technology b, MC_b.

It is to be noted that, since $\tau = -\frac{\partial c_i}{\partial r_i}$ then $\frac{\partial MC_i}{\partial \tau} = r_i$.

Furthermore, under taxes on consumers, $MC_i = c_i + r_i(0)\ \tau$ with $i = a,\ b$.

To simulate market power a dominant firm with fringe model is adopted.[3] The leader (d) is more efficient since it operates only the technology a with lower production costs. Consequently, $c_d = c_a$ and $r_d = r_a$. The fringe (f)[4] operates only the technology b with higher production costs and therefore it is the less efficient, $c_f = c_b$ and $r_f = r_b$.

The leader and the fringe supply the market with capacity $\bar{q}_d = \bar{q}_a > 0$ and $\bar{q}_f = \bar{q}_b > 0$ respectively. Their levels of production are $q_d \in [0; \bar{q}_a]$ and $q_f \in [0; \bar{q}_b]$ respectively. The firms' capacities are exogenous and the fringe is capacity constrained while the dominant firm is able to serve the entire market alone, $\bar{q}_d = Q(c_d)$ and $\bar{q}_f < Q(c_f)$.

[3] Several authors use this model in order to simulate the relationship between market power and environmental regulation. Among them: Conrad and Wang (1993), Chernyavs'ka and Gullì (2008), Gullì (2008), and Chernyavs'ka and Gullì (2009).

[4] It is to be noted that this model is well suited to simulate the structural features of several important environmentally regulated markets (e.g., energy markets).

Firms are price-setting and all players are assumed to be risk neutral and to act in order to maximize their expected payoff (profit). Production costs, emission rates as well as firms' installed capacity are common knowledge.

Throughout the analysis, efficient rationing is assumed. This means that, when the dominant firm (holding the most efficient technology) and the fringe set the same prices, the former serves the consumers first.

The indifference price of the input i, p_{n_i}, is that price which makes the final consumer indifferent when choosing between technology i and technology j.

For example, under symmetric taxes on consumers (input taxes applied to both the dominant and the fringe technologies), this price is obtained by solving the following equation

$$c_j + \tau\, r_j(0) = p_{n_i} + \tau\, r_i(0)$$

Then

$$p_{n_i} = c_j + \tau(r_j(0) - r_i(0))$$

Under symmetric taxes on producers, it is

$$p_{n_i} = c_j + \tau\, r_j(\tau)$$

and, since $\tau = -\partial c_j / \partial r_j$, then $\partial p_{n_i} / \partial \tau = r_j(\tau)$.

Finally if the prices of technology j are regulated and with ETS and free allocation of emissions allowances, we get

$$p_{n_i} = c_j + \tau\, r_j(\tau) - \tau\, r_{bn_j}\gamma$$

3 Impact on Pollution: Theoretical Analysis

By facing the fringe, the dominant firm will maximize its profit on the residual demand. Given the assumptions described in the previous section, this means that it will choose one of the following strategies: (1) setting prices above the indifference price so as to accommodate the fringe's maximum production (2) setting prices just below the indifference price and maximizing its market share.

By assumption, there will be an increase in market power when, because of the implementation of the environmental regulation, the dominant firm will move from the strategy (2) to the strategy (1). Inversely, there will be a decrease in market power if, because of the environmental regulation implementation, the dominant firm will move from strategy (1) to strategy (2).

The following Lemma describes the conditions under which the environmental regulation can decrease or increase market power.

Lemma 1. *(i) Under emissions taxes (or emissions trading) applied to the dominant firm, the environmental regulation can decrease market power if and only if*

$$d\Pi_u = \left(\frac{\partial p_{n_a}}{\partial \tau} - \frac{\partial MC_d}{\partial \tau}\right) - \alpha_1^2 \frac{\partial p_{n_a}}{\partial \tau} + \alpha_1 \frac{\partial MC_d}{\partial \tau} > 0 \tag{2.4}$$

where $\alpha_1 = \dfrac{(Q(p_r) - \bar{q}_f)}{Q(p_{n_a})}$ *and* $p_r = \arg\max_p \left[p(Q - \bar{q}_f) - C_d\right]$;

(ii) Inversely (increasing market power) when $d\Pi_u < 0$;

(iii) If $r_b < r_a$ *and* $\tau \geq \tau_s$ *then market power never decreases.*

Proof. See Appendix. The intuition is straightforward. For example, assume that $r_b < r_a$ and that, before the implementation of the environmental regulation, the dominant firm prefers to accommodate the fringe's maximum production. Neglecting the second-order terms, the first and second members of the right side of (2.4) represent the profit sensitivity of the dominant firm's strategy 2 (change in profit) per unit of dominant firm's maximum production. The second member is the profit sensitivity of the dominant firm's strategy 1 (loss of profit) per unit of dominant firm's maximum production. If the former is positive or, even if negative, is above the latter (the loss of profit of strategy 1 is lower than the loss of profit of strategy 2) then the dominant firm, after the environmental regulation implementation (and if the pollution price is enough high), will prefer to maximize its production. If the pollution price is very high, such that the leader becomes the less efficient firm (so losing its leadership cost), the latter strategy must be excluded.

Corollary 1. *If input taxes are applied to the dominant firm's consumers, the environmental regulation can decrease market power:*

(i) when input taxes are applied to both dominant firm's and fringe's consumers, if and only if

$$d\Pi_u = \left(\frac{\partial p_{n_a}}{\partial \tau} - \frac{\partial MC_d}{\partial \tau}\right) - \alpha_2^2 \left(\frac{\partial p_{n_a}}{\partial \tau} + r_b(0)\right) + \alpha_2 \left(\frac{\partial MC_d}{\partial \tau} + r_a(0)\right) > 0 \tag{2.5}$$

with $\alpha_2 = \dfrac{Q(p_r) - \bar{q}_f + r_a(0)\tau \partial Q/\partial p}{Q(p_{n_a}) + r_b(0)\tau \partial Q/\partial p}$

(ii) when input taxes are applied only to the dominant firm's consumers, if and only if

$$d\Pi_u = \left(\frac{\partial p_{n_a}}{\partial \tau} - \frac{\partial MC_d}{\partial \tau}\right) - \alpha_3^2 \frac{\partial p_{n_a}}{\partial \tau} + \alpha_3 \left(\frac{\partial MC_d}{\partial \tau} + r_a(0)\right) > 0 \tag{2.6}$$

with $\alpha_3 = \dfrac{Q(p_r) - \bar{q}_f + r_a(0)\tau \partial Q/\partial p}{Q(p_{n_a})}$;

Proof. See Appendix.

With increasing market power, before environmental policy ($\tau = 0$) the dominant firm (low-cost technology) serves the entire market:

$$\begin{cases} q_a(0) = Q(c_b) \\ q_b(0) = 0 \end{cases}$$

If τ is sufficiently high, after the environmental regulation, the dominant firm prefers to accommodate the fringe technology:

$$\begin{cases} q_a(\tau) = Q(\hat{p}_r(\tau)) - \bar{q}_f \\ q_b(\tau) = \bar{q}_f \end{cases}$$

where $\hat{p}_r = p_r$ under taxes on producers. Under taxes on consumers, $\hat{p}_r$ is the monopoly price on the net residual demand (net of the portion of demand corresponding to the increase in price due to the tax rate applied to consumers, see Appendix) plus the tax on consumers.

Then the change in pollution is:

$$\Delta E = r_b(\tau)\bar{q}_f + r_a(\tau)\left[Q(\hat{p}_r(\tau)) - \bar{q}_f\right] - r_a(0)Q(c_b) \tag{2.7}$$

Consequently, $\Delta E > 0$ if

$$\Delta E_{u_1} = \frac{\Delta E}{\bar{q}_f} = r_b(\tau) + r_a(\tau)\frac{\left[Q(\hat{p}_r(\tau)) - \bar{q}_f\right]}{\bar{q}_f} - r_a(0)\frac{Q(c_b)}{\bar{q}_f} > 0 \tag{2.8}$$

This condition is never satisfied if $r_b < r_a$. If $r_b > r_a$ it may be satisfied when the difference in emission rates between technologies is high (large environmental asymmetry of firms) and/or the price elasticity of demand is very low and abatement technologies are relatively inefficient.

Under imperfect competition and with decreasing market power, before the environmental policy ($\tau = 0$) the fringe exploits its maximum capacity and the dominant firm (operating the low-cost technology) supplies the residual demand:

$$\begin{cases} q_a(0) = Q(p_r(0)) - \bar{q}_f \\ q_b(0) = \bar{q}_f \end{cases}$$

If τ is sufficiently high, after the environmental regulation the dominant firm prefers to maximize its production:

$$\begin{cases} q_a(\tau) = Q(\hat{c}_b) \\ q_b(\tau) = 0 \end{cases}$$

The change in emissions is

$$\Delta E = r_a(\tau)(Q(\hat{c}_b) - r_a(0)\left[Q(p_r(0)) - \bar{q}_f\right] - r_b(0)\bar{q}_f \quad (2.9)$$

Then $\Delta E > 0$ if

$$\Delta E_{u_2} = \frac{\Delta E}{\bar{q}_f} = r_a(\tau)\frac{Q(\hat{c}_b)}{\bar{q}_f} - r_a(0)\frac{\left[Q(p_r(0)) - \bar{q}_f\right]}{\bar{q}_f} - r_b(0) > 0 \quad (2.10)$$

where $\hat{c}_b = c_b + r_b(\tau)\tau$ under emissions taxes on fringe's producers, $\hat{c}_b = c_b + r_b(0)\tau$ under input taxes on fringe's consumers and $\hat{c}_b = c_b + (r_b(\tau) - r_{bn_b}\gamma)\tau$ under ETS with free allocation and pricing regulation.

This condition is satisfied if $r_b < r_a$ and abatement technologies are relatively inefficient. If $r_b > r_a$ it may be satisfied especially when the difference in emission rates between technologies is low and/or the price elasticity of demand is relatively high and abatement technologies are relatively inefficient.

The results described above can be summarized as follows:

Lemma 2. *(i) If $r_b < r_a$ decreasing market power is necessary condition for increasing pollution; (ii) If $r_b > r_a$ the outcome is ambiguous.*

Proof. See (2.7)–(2.10).

Given Lemma 2, the probability of increasing pollution can be estimated by using condition (2.4) [or (2.5) or (2.6)] and conditions (2.8) and (2.10) simultaneously.

In the following Subsections, firstly symmetric regulation will be taken into account (the same environmental tool applied to different supply technologies). Subsequently, hybrid solutions will be investigated (different environmental tools applied to the different technological solutions).

3.1 Symmetric Regulation

Symmetric regulation arises when the same environmental tool is applied to different technologies.

3.1.1 Symmetric Taxes on Consumers

In this case pollution taxes are directly applied to the input purchased by final consumers. For example, if the space heating technology is based on the use of natural gas boilers, taxes are charged to natural gas consumption (monetary charge per unit of natural gas consumed).

However, it is reasonable to assume that policymakers choose the input tax by looking at the emissions rate before the implementation of environmental regulation. Therefore, the input tax can be expressed as $\tau\ r_i(0)$.

Under symmetric taxes on consumers, the indifference price is obtained by solving the following equation:

$$c_b + \tau\ r_b(0) = p_{n_a} + \tau\ r_a(0)$$

Then

$$p_{n_a} = c_b + \tau(r_b(0) - r_a(0))$$

Since $\frac{\partial c_b}{\partial \tau} = 0$, the dominant firm's indifference price sensitivity to pollution price will be

$$\frac{\partial p_{n_a}}{\partial \tau} = r_b(0) - r_a(0)$$

and, since no tax is applied to producers, the dominant firm's cost sensitivity to pollution price will be

$$\frac{\partial MC_d}{\partial \tau} = 0$$

Then from Corollary 1 (2.5), the condition for decreasing market power is:

$$r_b(0) > r_a(0)\frac{1 - \alpha_2^2 - \alpha_2}{1 - 2\alpha_2^2}$$

If $r_b < r_a$ decreasing market power is admissible provided that the difference in emissions rates is very low. Therefore, increasing pollution is admissible although it seems to be unlikely.

If $r_b > r_a$ it is very likely that $d\Pi_u > 0$. Consequently, from condition (2.10), increasing pollution is admissible when the difference in emission rates between technologies is low and/or the price elasticity of demand is high provided that abatement technologies are sufficiently inefficient.

3.1.2 Symmetric Taxes on Producers (or ETS with Auctioning)

In this case, taxes are applied to producers and are proportional to emissions. This time the emissions rate depends on the pollution price. It is also to be noted that taxes on producers are equivalent to ETS with auctioning.

Under symmetric taxes on producers (or symmetric ETS with auctioning), the indifference price is

$$p_{n_a} = c_b(\tau) + \tau\, r_b(\tau)$$

Since from (2.3) $\tau = -\dfrac{\partial c_b}{\partial r_b}$, the indifference price sensitivity to pollution price is

$$\frac{\partial p_{n_a}}{\partial \tau} = r_b(\tau)$$

and, since $\tau = -\dfrac{\partial c_a}{\partial r_a}$, the dominant firm's cost sensitivity to pollution price is:

$$\frac{\partial MC_d}{\partial \tau} = r_a(\tau)$$

Then from Lemma 1, the condition for decreasing market power is

$$r_b(\tau) > r_a(\tau)\frac{1}{1+\alpha_1}$$

Therefore, if $r_b < r_a$ increasing pollution is admissible provided that abatement technologies are relatively inefficient.

If $r_b > r_a$ the condition for decreasing market power is satisfied always. Pollution can increase if the difference in emissions rates is low and abatement technologies are sufficiently inefficient.

It is to be noted that $1/(1+\alpha_1)$ may be lower than $(1-\alpha_2^2-\alpha_2)/(1-2\alpha_2^2)$ when $\alpha_2 < \alpha_1$. Since this always occurs if $r_b < r_a$ then decreasing market power (and consequently increasing pollution) might be more likely under taxes on producers than under taxes on consumers. When $r_b > r_a$ this can occur if the difference in emissions rate is relatively low. Otherwise (sufficiently large environmental asymmetry) increasing emissions is more likely with taxes on consumers.

3.1.3 Symmetric ETS with Free Allocation of Emissions Allowances

Under ETS with free allocation, emissions allowances are allocated free of charge to polluters. The amount of these allowances (expressed in terms of emissions) is equal to the reference emissions rate multiplied by the reference level of production.

In this case it is necessary to distinguish two scenarios of fringe's technology pricing: unregulated prices and regulated prices.

When unregulated, fringe's prices converge to marginal costs. Therefore

$$p_{n_a} = c_b(\tau) + \tau\, r_b(\tau)$$

and, since $\tau = -\frac{\partial c_b}{\partial r_b}$, the fringe's indifference price sensitivity to pollution price is:

$$\frac{\partial p_{n_a}}{\partial \tau} = r_b(\tau)$$

At the same time, since $\tau = -\frac{\partial c_a}{\partial r_a}$, the dominant firm's marginal cost sensitivity to pollution price will be:

$$\frac{\partial MC_d}{\partial \tau} = r_a(\tau)$$

Consequently, from Lemma 1 (2.4) the condition for decreasing market power is

$$r_b(\tau) > r_a(\tau)\frac{1}{1+\alpha_1}$$

Therefore, if $r_b < r_a$ increasing pollution is admissible provided that abatement technologies are not particularly efficient.

If $r_b > r_a$ the condition for decreasing market power is satisfied always. Pollution can increase if the difference in emissions rates is low and abatement technologies are sufficiently inefficient.

Under regulated prices, when prices are equal to the average production cost, the fringe's indifference price is obtained by solving the following equation [from (2.2)]:

$$p_{n_a} = c_b(\tau) + \tau\, r_b(\tau) - \tau\, r_{bn_b}\gamma$$

Then by differentiating the previous equation and given that $\tau = -\frac{\partial c_b}{\partial r_b}$, the indifference price sensitivity will be

$$\frac{\partial p_{n_a}}{\partial \tau} = r_b(\tau) - r_{bn_b}\gamma$$

It is to be noted that γ does not depend on pollution price. In fact we assume that the sector-specific authority set regulated prices by looking at the production level before the change in pollution price (or before the implementation of the environmental policy)

The dominant firm's cost sensitivity to pollution price is

$$\frac{\partial MC_d}{\partial \tau} = r_a(\tau)$$

Consequently, the condition for decreasing market power (from Lemma 1) becomes

$$r_b(\tau) > r_a(\tau)\frac{1}{1+\alpha_1} + r_{bn_b}\gamma$$

If $r_b < r_a$, decreasing market power and increasing pollution are admissible. However they seem to be very unlikely, at least in principle.

If $r_b > r_a$, the condition for decreasing market power is satisfied if the difference in emissions rates is relatively high. However, in this case, increasing pollution is very unlikely [see (2.10)]. Inversely, market power can increase if

$$r_b(\tau) < r_a(\tau)\frac{1}{1+\alpha_1} + r_{bn_b}\gamma$$

This condition is satisfied if the difference in emissions rates is low. However, this drastically reduces the probability of increasing pollution.

In conclusion, increasing pollution seems to be very unlikely.

3.2 *Hybrid Regulation*

Hybrid regulation arises when different environmental tools are applied to different competing technologies.

3.2.1 Taxes on Consumers Versus Taxes on Producers (or ETS with Auctioning)

Two cases have to be analyzed: (1) taxes on the dominant firm's consumers and taxes on the fringe's producers (or ETS with auctioning); (2) taxes on the fringe's consumers and taxes on the dominant firm's producers (or ETS with auctioning).

In the first case, the indifference price sensitivity to pollution price is

$$\frac{\partial p_{n_a}}{\partial \tau} = r_b(\tau) - r_a(0)$$

and the dominant firm's cost sensitivity to pollution price is

$$\frac{\partial MC_d}{\partial \tau} = 0$$

Consequently, from Corollary 1 (2.6):

$$r_b(\tau) > r_a(0)\frac{1-\alpha_3^2-\alpha_3}{1-\alpha_3^2}$$

If $r_b < r_a$ market power can decrease provided that the environmental asymmetry between firms is sufficiently restricted. Therefore, increasing pollution is admissible.

If $r_b > r_a$ then $d\Pi_u > 0$ always. However, increasing pollution is admissible when the difference in emission rates between technologies is low and/or the price elasticity of demand is sufficiently high provided that abatement technologies are sufficiently inefficient.

It is to be noted that $1/(1+\alpha_1)$ may be lower than $(1-\alpha_3^2-\alpha_3)/(1-\alpha_3^2)$ when $\alpha_3 < \alpha_1$. Since this always occurs always (regardless of whether $r_b < r_a$ or $r_b > r_a$) then decreasing market power (and consequently increasing pollution) might be more likely under taxes on producers than under taxes on consumers.

In the second case:

$$\frac{\partial p_{n_a}}{\partial \tau} = r_b(0)$$

and

$$\frac{\partial MC_d}{\partial \tau} = r_a(\tau)$$

The condition for decreasing market power (2.4) is

$$r_b(0) > r_a(\tau)\frac{1}{1+\alpha_1}$$

Therefore, if $r_b < r_a$, increasing pollution is admissible. If $r_b > r_a$, this condition is always satisfied. Increasing pollution is admissible provided that the difference in emissions rate is low, abatement technologies are inefficient, and the price elasticity of demand is high.

It is to be noted that, this time, decreasing market power (and consequently increasing pollution) may be more likely under taxes on consumers than under taxes on producers.

3.2.2 Taxes on Producers (or ETS with Auctioning) Versus ETS with Free Allocation of Emissions Allowances

Three relevant combinations of environmental regulation have to be analyzed: (1) taxes on dominant firm's production (or ETS with auctioning) and ETS with free allocation on fringe's producers with unregulated fringe's prices; (2) taxes on dominant firm's production (or ETS with auctioning) and ETS with free allocation on fringe's producers with regulated fringe's prices; (3) ETS on dominant firm production and taxes on fringe's producers (or ETS with auctioning).

In the first case, the indifference price sensitivity to pollution price is:

$$\frac{\partial p_{n_a}}{\partial \tau} = r_b(\tau)$$

and the dominant firm's cost sensitivity to pollution price is

$$\frac{\partial MC_d}{\partial \tau} = r_a(\tau)$$

Consequently, the result is the same than under symmetric taxes on producers. The condition for decreasing market power (2.4) is:

$$r_b(\tau) > r_a(\tau)\frac{1}{1+\alpha_1}$$

If $r_b < r_a$, decreasing market power and increasing pollution are admissible.

If $r_b > r_a$, market power decreases always. Increasing pollution is admissible if the difference in emissions rates is low and abatement technologies are inefficient and price elasticity of demand is high.

In the second case, the indifference price sensitivity to pollution price is

$$\frac{\partial p_{n_a}}{\partial \tau} = r_b(\tau) - r_{bn_b}\gamma$$

The dominant firm's cost sensitivity to pollution price is

$$\frac{\partial MC_d}{\partial \tau} = r_a(\tau)$$

Consequently, the condition for decreasing market power (2.4) becomes:

$$r_b(\tau) > r_a(\tau)\frac{1}{1+\alpha_1} + r_{bn_b}\gamma$$

If $r_b < r_a$, increasing pollution is admissible but very unlikely.

If $r_b > r_a$, market power decreases only if the difference in emissions rates is high. However, in this case, the probability of increasing pollution is low. Inversely, increasing market power is likely if the difference in emissions rates is low. Once again this reduces the probability of increasing pollution. In conclusion, increasing pollution is admissible but very unlikely.

Finally, in the third case

$$\frac{\partial p_{n_a}}{\partial \tau} = r_b(\tau)$$

and the dominant firm's cost sensitivity to pollution price is

$$\frac{\partial MC_d}{\partial \tau} = r_a(\tau)$$

Consequently, the condition for increasing pollution (2.4) is

$$r_b(\tau) > r_a(\tau)\frac{1}{1+\alpha_1}$$

If $r_b < r_a$, increasing pollution is admissible. If $r_b > r_a$, this condition is satisfied always. Therefore, increasing pollution is admissible provided that the difference in emissions rate is low and abatement technologies are inefficient.

3.2.3 Taxes on Consumers Versus ETS with Free Allocation of Emissions Allowances

Three relevant hybrid combinations arise: (1) taxes on the dominant firm's consumers and ETS with free allocation to fringe's producers, when fringe's prices are unregulated; (2) taxes on the dominant firm's consumers and ETS with free allocation to the fringe's consumers, when fringe's prices are regulated; (3) taxes on fringe's consumers and ETS with free allocation to the dominant firm's producers.

In the first case

$$\frac{\partial p_{n_a}}{\partial \tau} = r_b(\tau) - r_a(0)$$

and $\dfrac{\partial MC_d}{\partial \tau} = 0$. Then from Corollary 1 (2.6):

$$r_b(\tau) > r_a(0)\frac{1-\alpha_3^2-\alpha_3}{1-\alpha_3^2}$$

If $r_b < r_a$, market power can decrease if the difference in emissions rates is low. Therefore, increasing pollution is admissible.

If $r_b > r_a$, then this condition is always satisfied ($d\Pi_u > 0$ always). Consequently, increasing pollution is admissible. However, this requires that the difference in emission rates between technologies is low and/or the price elasticity of demand is high. Furthermore, abatement technologies must be sufficiently inefficient.

In the second case,

$$\frac{\partial p_{n_a}}{\partial \tau} = r_b(\tau) - r_{bn_b}\gamma - r_a(0)$$

and $\frac{\partial MC_d}{\partial \tau} = 0$. Then, from (2.6) the condition for decreasing market power becomes:

$$r_b(\tau) > r_a(0)\frac{1 - \alpha_3^2 - \alpha_3}{1 - \alpha_3^2} + r_{bn_b}\gamma$$

Therefore, if $r_b < r_a$, increasing pollution is admissible but very unlikely. If $r_b > r_a$, it is admissible. However, the condition for decreasing market power is satisfied if the difference in emissions rates is very high. But in this case the probability of increasing pollution is very low. Inversely, market power increases if the difference in emissions rates is very low. Once again, this drastically reduces the probability of increasing pollution. In conclusion, increasing emissions is very unlikely.

In the third case, this time taxes are directly charged to the fringe's consumers. The indifference price is

$$\frac{\partial p_{n_a}}{\partial \tau} = r_b(0)$$

and

$$\frac{\partial MC_d}{\partial \tau} = r_a(\tau)$$

The condition for decreasing market power (2.4) is

$$r_b(0) > r_a(\tau)\frac{1}{1 + \alpha_1}$$

If $r_b < r_a$, increasing pollution is admissible. If $r_b > r_a$, this condition is satisfied always. Therefore, market power decreases always. This leads to increased pollution if the difference in emissions rates is low and abatement technologies are inefficient and price elasticity of demand is high.

3.3 The Overall Framework

Tables 2.1, 2.2, and 2.3 summarize the results described in the previous Subsections. Table 2.1 reports the parameters used to calculate the probability of increasing or decreasing market power. Tables 2.2 and 2.3 summarize the probability of increasing pollution in qualitative terms.

The following considerations arise:

1. Increasing pollution is admissible in principle. Furthermore, it does not require large (environmental) asymmetry of firms. Rather in most cases low asymmetry of firms is necessary.
2. Increasing pollution might be less likely under input taxes on consumers than under emission taxes (or ETS with auctioning) on producers.

Table 2.1 Parameters

	Dominant firm		
Fringe	Taxes on consumers	Taxes on producers or ETS with auctioning	ETS with free allocation
Taxes on consumers	$\frac{\partial p_{n_a}}{\partial \tau} = r_b(0) - r_a(0)$	$\frac{\partial p_{n_a}}{\partial \tau} = r_b(0)$	$\frac{\partial p_{n_a}}{\partial \tau} = r_b(0)$
	$\frac{\partial MC_d}{\partial \tau} = 0$	$\frac{\partial MC_d}{\partial \tau} = r_a(\tau)$	$\frac{\partial MC_d}{\partial \tau} = r_a(\tau)$
Taxes on producers or ETS with auctioning	$\frac{\partial p_{n_a}}{\partial \tau} = r_b(\tau) - r_a(0)$	$\frac{\partial p_{n_a}}{\partial \tau} = r_b(\tau)$	$\frac{\partial p_{n_a}}{\partial \tau} = r_b(\tau)$
	$\frac{\partial MC_d}{\partial \tau} = 0$	$\frac{\partial MC_d}{\partial \tau} = r_a(\tau)$	$\frac{\partial MC_d}{\partial \tau} = r_a(\tau)$
ETS with free allocation (unregulated prices)	$\frac{\partial p_{n_a}}{\partial \tau} = r_b(\tau) - r_a(0)$	$\frac{\partial p_{n_a}}{\partial \tau} = r_b(\tau)$	$\frac{\partial p_{n_a}}{\partial \tau} = r_b(\tau)$
	$\frac{\partial MC_d}{\partial \tau} = 0$	$\frac{\partial MC_d}{\partial \tau} = r_a(\tau)$	$\frac{\partial MC_d}{\partial \tau} = r_a(\tau)$
ETS with free allocation (regulated prices)	$\frac{\partial p_{n_a}}{\partial \tau} = r_b(\tau) - r_{bn_b}\gamma - r_a(0)$	$\frac{\partial p_{n_a}}{\partial \tau} = r_b(\tau) - r_{bn_b}\gamma$	$\frac{\partial p_{n_a}}{\partial \tau} = r_b(\tau) - r_{bn_b}\gamma$
	$\frac{\partial MC_d}{\partial \tau} = 0$	$\frac{\partial MC_d}{\partial \tau} = r_a(\tau)$	$\frac{\partial MC_d}{\partial \tau} = r_a(\tau)$

Table 2.2 Probability of increasing pollution $(r_b < r_a)$

	Dominant firm		
Fringe	Taxes on consumers	Taxes on producers or ETS with auctioning	ETS with free allocation
Taxes on consumers	Admissible (low environmental asymmetry)	Admissible	Admissible
Taxes on producers or ETS with auctioning	Admissible (low environmental asymmetry)	Admissible	Admissible
ETS with free allocation (unregulated prices)	Admissible (low environmental asymmetry)	Admissible	Admissible
ETS with free allocation (regulated prices)	Admissible (very unlikely)	Admissible (very unlikely)	Admissible (very unlikely)

Table 2.3 Probability of increasing pollution $(r_b > r_a)$

	Dominant firm		
Fringe	Taxes on consumers	Taxes on producers or ETS with auctioning	ETS with free allocation
Taxes on consumers	Admissible (low environmental asymmetry)	Admissible (low environmental asymmetry)	Admissible (low environmental asymmetry)
Taxes on producers or ETS with auctioning	Admissible (low environmental asymmetry)	Admissible (low environmental asymmetry)	Admissible (low environmental asymmetry)
ETS with free allocation (unregulated prices)	Admissible (low environmental asymmetry)	Admissible (low environmental asymmetry)	Admissible (low environmental asymmetry)
ETS with free allocation (regulated prices)	Admissible (very unlikely)	Admissible (very unlikely)	Admissible (very unlikely)

3. Free allocation of emissions allowances combined with pricing regulation drastically reduces the probability of increasing pollution.
4. Hybrid regulation can play a significant role in affecting the probability that environmental policy could lead to increased emissions. Nevertheless, this role is ambiguous. Compared to symmetric regulation, hybrid regulation can increase or decrease the probability of increasing pollution depending on several factors.
5. Increasing pollution (where admissible) seems to be relatively likely in several situations where the dominant technology is highly polluting (more polluting than the fringe technology).

The main findings are summarized by the following proposition and corollary.

Proposition 1. *(i) Increasing pollution is widely admissible in principle. (ii) Its probability might be lower with input taxes on consumers and (ii) decreases with free allocation of emissions allowances. (iii) The role of hybrid regulation is significant but ambiguous.*

Proof. See Tables 2.2 and 2.3.

Finally, it is to be noted that, if the dominant technology is more polluting than the fringe one, increasing pollution is admissible and seems to be likely, unless input taxes are applied to the dominant firm's consumers.

This result suggests that when polarized configurations are due to energy policies promoting the deployment of cleaner technologies (fringe technologies), the implementation of environmental regulation may lead to a dual perverse effect. This may increase the risk that the dominant firm prefers to undercut the cleaner technology rather than to accommodate its production at the same time leading to increasing rather than decreasing pollution.

4 Impact on Pollution: Simulations

The analysis described above highlights that increasing pollution is admissible in principle in most combinations of environmental regulation. A last question remains: where admissible, how much is it really likely?

To answer this question, it is helpful to carry out the simulation of the typical cases of space heating which can be appropriately described by the dominant firm with fringe model.

Three possible technological solutions (natural gas boilers, district heating, and electric heat pumps) are simulated:

1. Natural gas fired boiler (technology 1). When this cycle is used, most part of pollution occurs in the consumption stage. This is the reasons why the most likely environmental regulation of this cycle is based on taxes applied to consumers (input taxes on natural gas consumption).
2. Combined Heat and Power (CHP) district heating using natural gas (technology 2). In this case, the useful heat for space heating is produced by a CHP plant located

Table 2.4 Technical parameters used for simulations (*)

		Natural gas boiler (1)	District Heating (CHP-gas) (2)	Electric Heat Pump (3)
$\bar{r}_i(0)$	tCO_2/MWh	0.30	0.20	0.10
c_a	€/MWh		30	
c_a/c_a			1.0	
c_b/c_a			1.5	
σ_b	tCO_2/MWh		0.05	
Cost function			$MC_i/c_a = c_i/c_a + (r_i\tau)/c_a$	
Emission rate function			$r_b(\tau) = \bar{r}_b(0) \cdot \exp(-0.007 \cdot \tau)$ $r_a(\tau) = \bar{r}_a(0) \cdot \exp(-0.01 \cdot \tau)$	
r_{bn_i}	tCO_2/MWh		$\bar{r}_i(0)$	
γ			0.8	
$\bar{q}_f$			$0.3 \cdot Q(c_a/c_a)$	
Inverse demand function			$p/c_a = 4 - 0.5 \cdot Q(p/c_a)$	

(*) Parameters account for the energy conversion efficiency (the ratio between the useful heat and the input)

relatively far from the consumers. Then the generated heat is transported over relatively long distances by means of a grid of pipelines and delivered to final consumers. Most pollution is concentrated in the generation stage (by the CHP plant). Therefore, almost all environmental tools can be applied. However, ETS with free allocation of allowances is most likely (this is the regulation adopted by the EU-ETS). In this case, we assume that the advantage due to free allocation is entirely attributed to heat production.

3. Heat pump using electricity generated by gas-fired power installations (technology 3). This typology of heat supply provides significant energy savings. The useful heat is produced by converting electricity in the consumption stage. Pollution is concentrated in the generation (power generation) stage. The efficiency of this cycle is given by the COP (Coefficient of Performance) which is equal to the useful heat produced divided by the electricity consumption of the heat pump. Even in this case, almost all environmental tools can be applied; however, ETS with auctioning of emissions allowances is the most likely of them. Finally, for the sake of simplicity, it is assumed that the power spot market (including only gas-fired power plants) is entirely "dedicated" to serve the space heating market.

Table 2.4 reports the technical and economic parameters related to each technology analyzed.

Given a specific technology, it is assumed that the fringe's emission rate is distributed normally around the corresponding mean value with a standard deviation σ_b. This distribution allows us to account for the dispersion of energy efficiency of different technological solutions: the dispersion of the electric efficiency of CHP district heating and power installations; the different possible coefficient of performance (COP) of electric heat pumps; the dispersion of thermal efficiency of gas-fired boilers.

The probability of increasing pollution is estimated by using the following procedure. In the same graph the condition for change in market power ($d\Pi_u$) and the condition for change in pollution (ΔE_u) are depicted (in terms of cumulative distributions). If the former is positive (negative), decreasing (increasing) market power is admissible. If the latter is positive (negative), increasing (decreasing) pollution is admissible. Then increasing pollution will occur when $d\Pi_u < 0$ combines with $\Delta E_{u_1} > 0$ or when $d\Pi_u > 0$ combines with $\Delta E_{u_2} > 0$. Obviously, since $d\Pi_u > 0$ (decreasing market power) is necessary condition for increasing pollution when $r_b < r_a$, in this case the probability of increasing emissions can be estimated by depicting just the probability of change in pollution when market power decreases (2.10). Furthermore, if $r_b < r_a$ and $d\Pi_u < 0$ always, pollution never increases.

By using this procedure, the expressions in Table 2.1 and the values in Table 2.4, the cumulative distributions illustrated in Figs. 2.1, 2.2, 2.3, 2.4, 2.5, and 2.6 follow.

These figures suggest the following considerations:

1. When the natural gas boiler is the dominant technology, there is a significant probability of increasing pollution only when the fringe technology is district heating and provided that the fringe's prices are not regulated. If the fringe technology is heat pump, increasing pollution is excluded or very unlikely. This confirms the theoretical findings. In fact, the most likely regulation of natural gas cycles is based on taxes on consumers since most part of pollution is concentrated in the stage of natural gas conversion to useful heat (by means of heat boilers directly exploited by consumers purchasing the energy input). Therefore, the numerical simulations confirm that under input taxes on consumers the probability of increasing emissions may be relatively low, especially if the dominant technology is more polluting than the fringe one.
2. When district heating is the dominant technology, increasing pollution is relatively likely under all combinations of environmental regulation. If the fringe technology is the natural gas boiler ($r_b > r_a$), the probability of increasing pollution is higher under symmetric taxes on consumers than under taxes on producers. If the fringe technology is heat pump ($r_b < r_a$), increasing pollution is less likely under symmetric taxes on consumers than under symmetric taxes on producers. These results confirm the theoretical predictions.
3. If the electric heat pump is the dominant technology, increasing pollution is excluded or very unlikely in all combinations of technologies and regulation.
4. Overall increasing pollution is virtually excluded or very unlikely in many situations where it is admissible in principle.
5. The numerical simulations also confirm that increasing pollution, where admissible, is more likely when the environmental asymmetry between firms is low. In fact the probability of increasing pollution becomes positive for high values of the cumulative distributions if $r_b < r_a$ (these values correspond to low difference

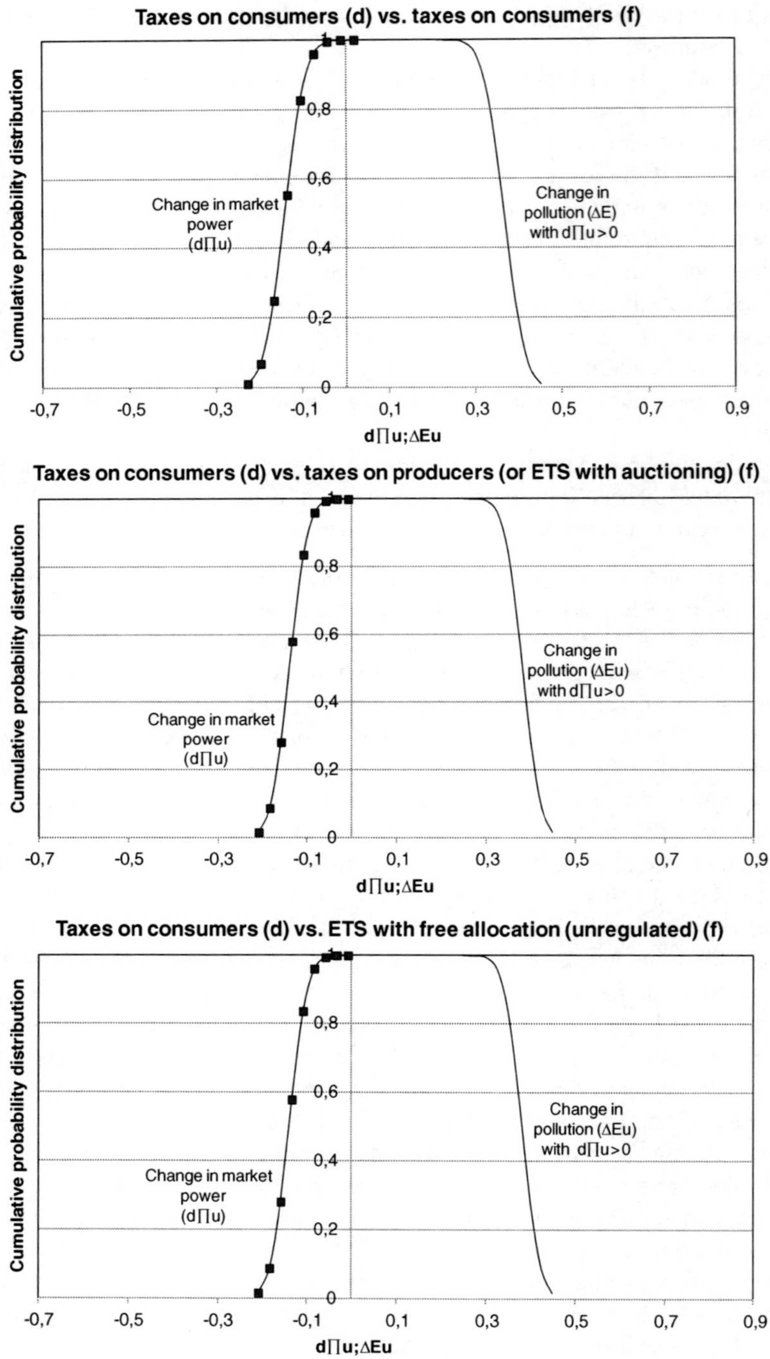

Fig. 2.1 Natural gas boiler (*d*) vs. heat pump (f) ($r_b < r_a$)

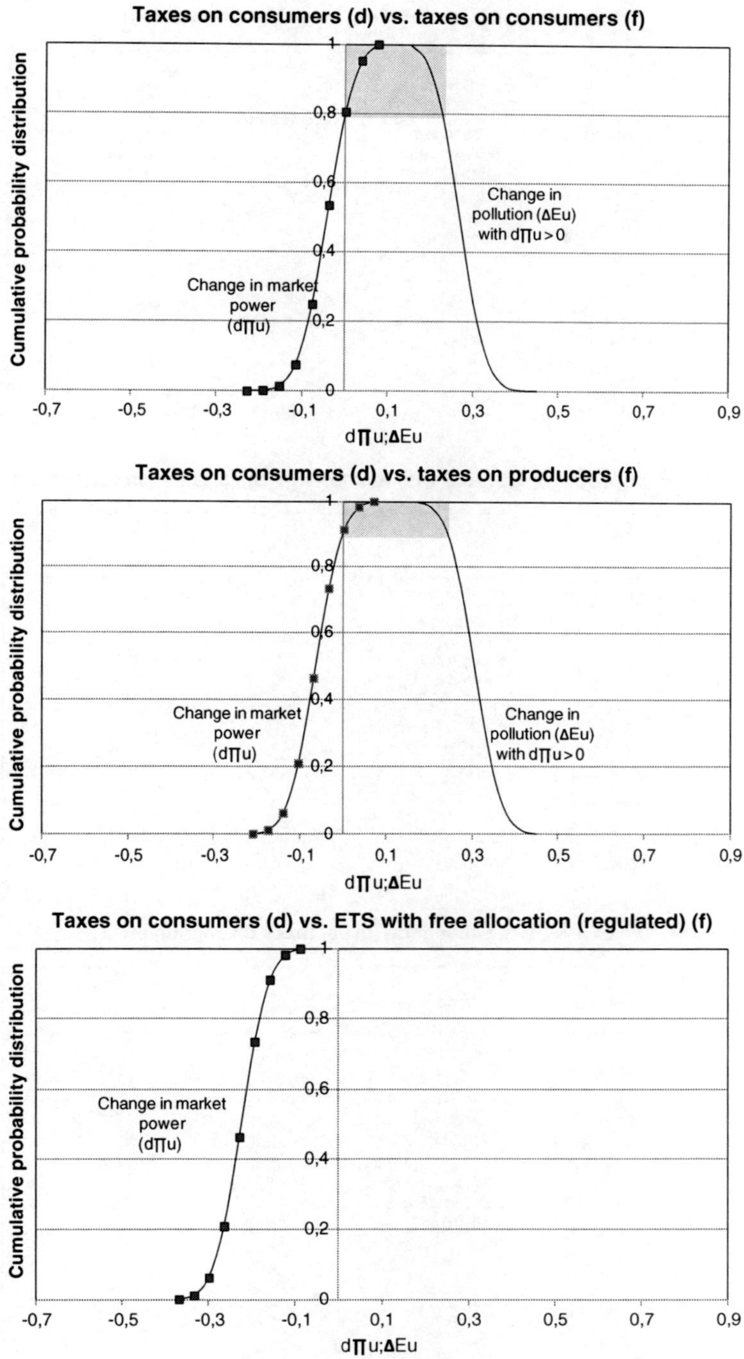

Fig. 2.2 Natural gas boiler (*d*) vs. district heating (f) ($r_b < r_a$)

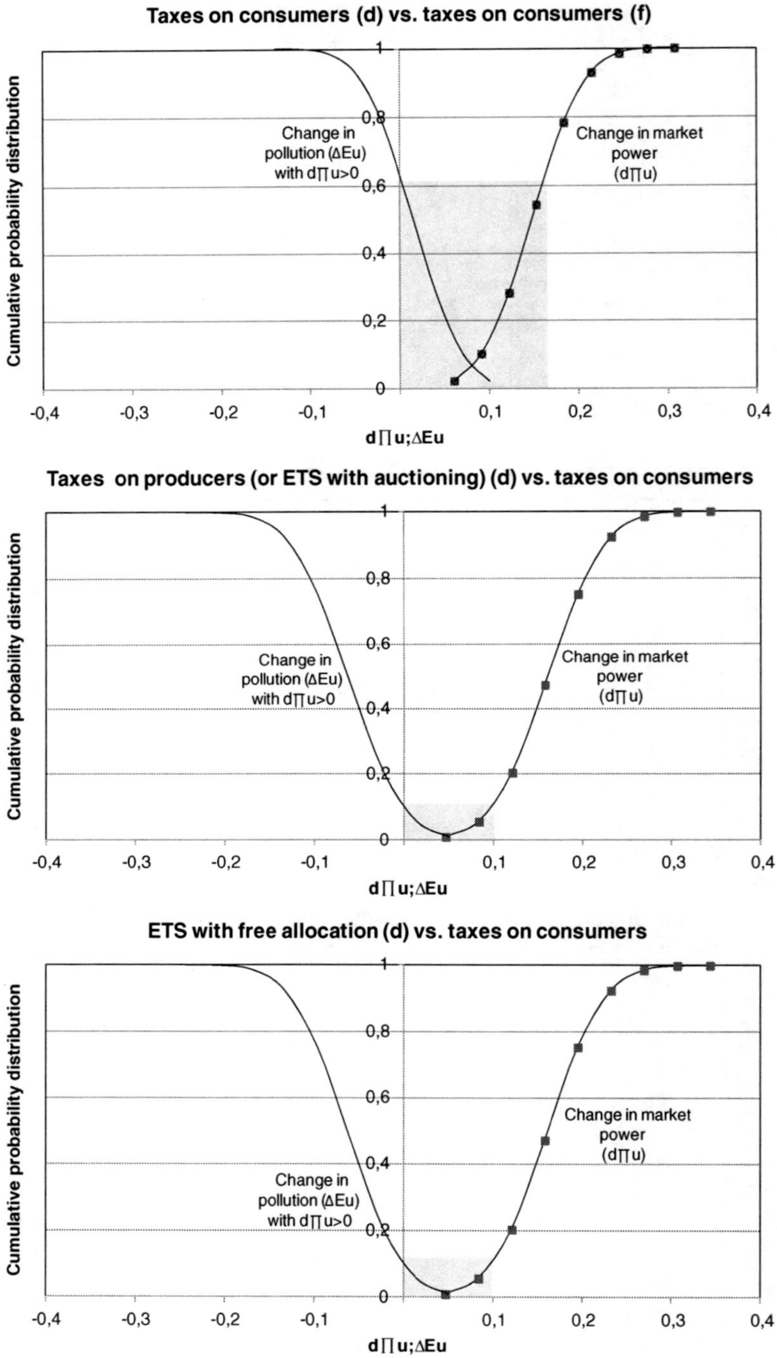

Fig. 2.3 District heating (d) vs. natural gas boiler (f) ($r_b > r_a$)

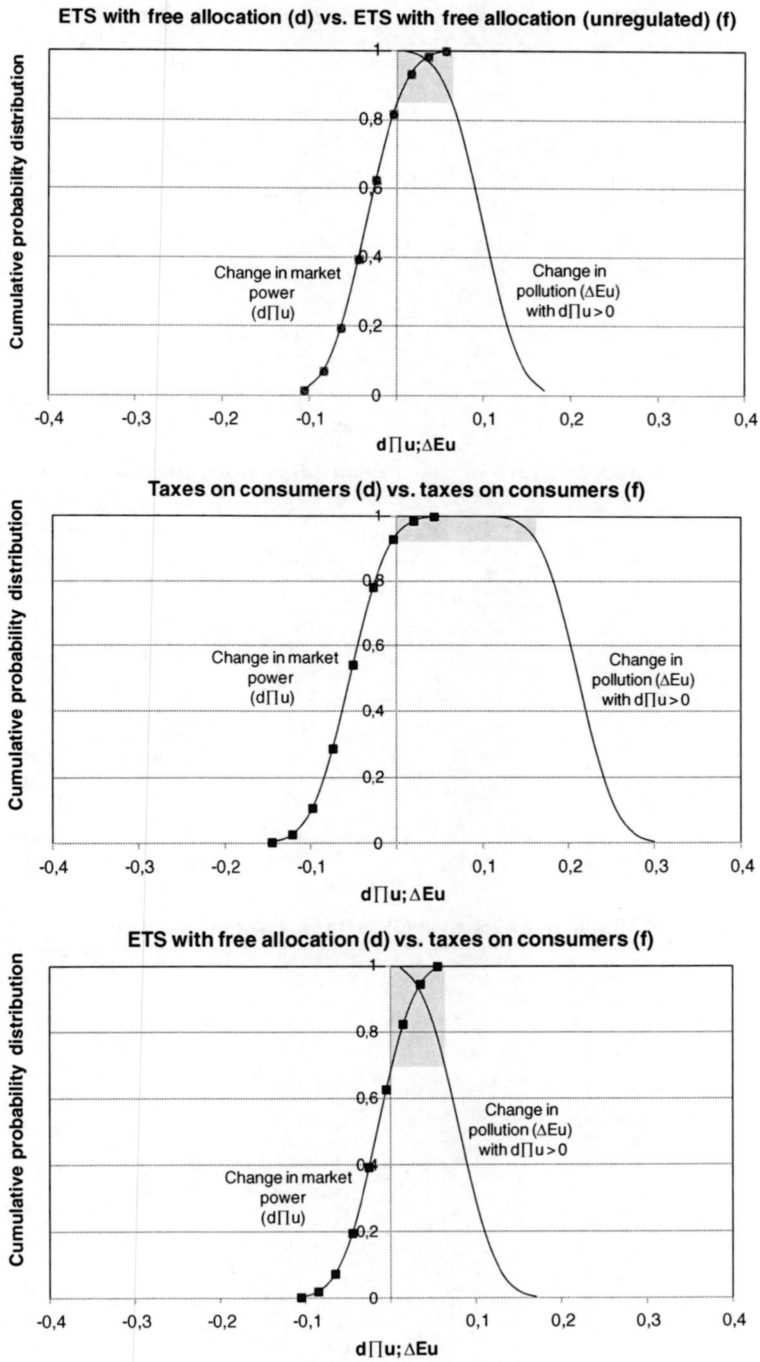

Fig. 2.4 District heating (*d*) vs. heat pump (f) ($r_b < r_a$)

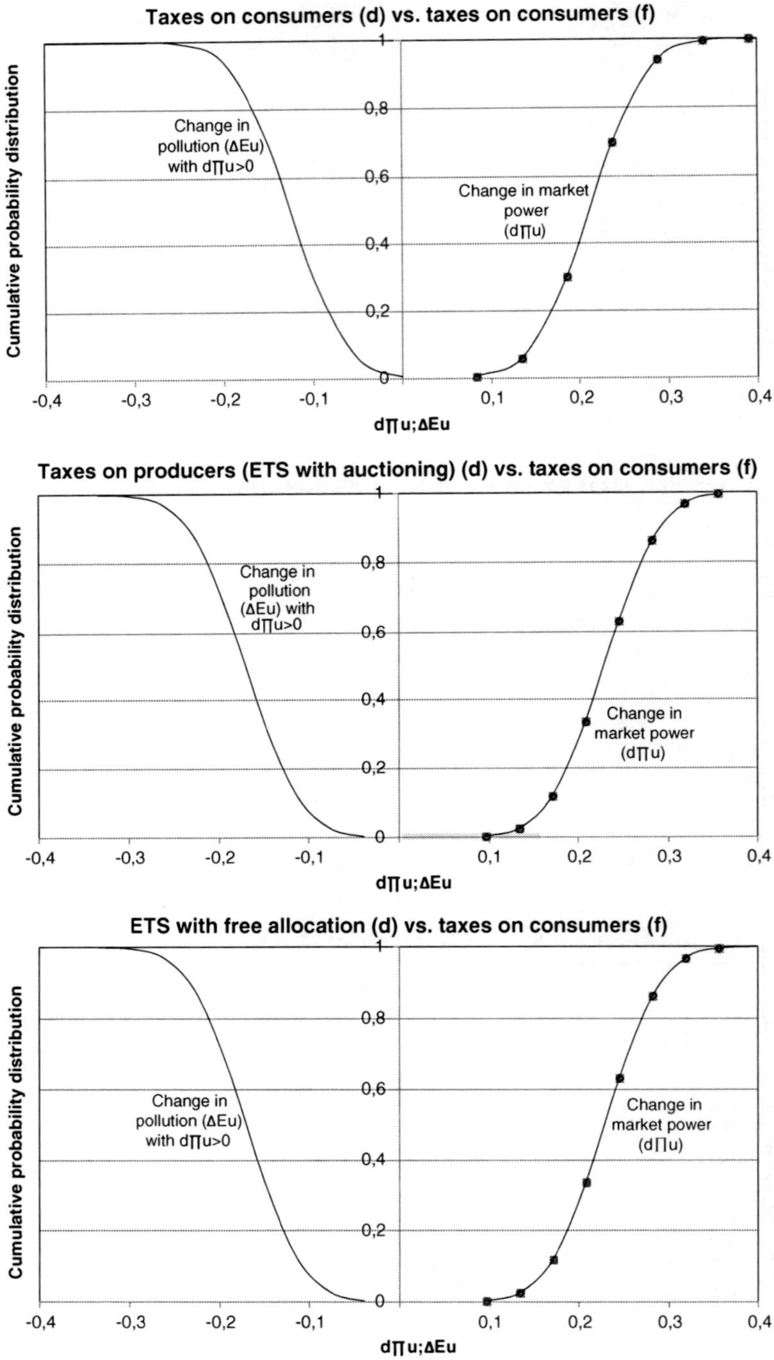

Fig. 2.5 Heat pump (*d*) vs. natural gas boiler (*f*) ($r_b > r_a$)

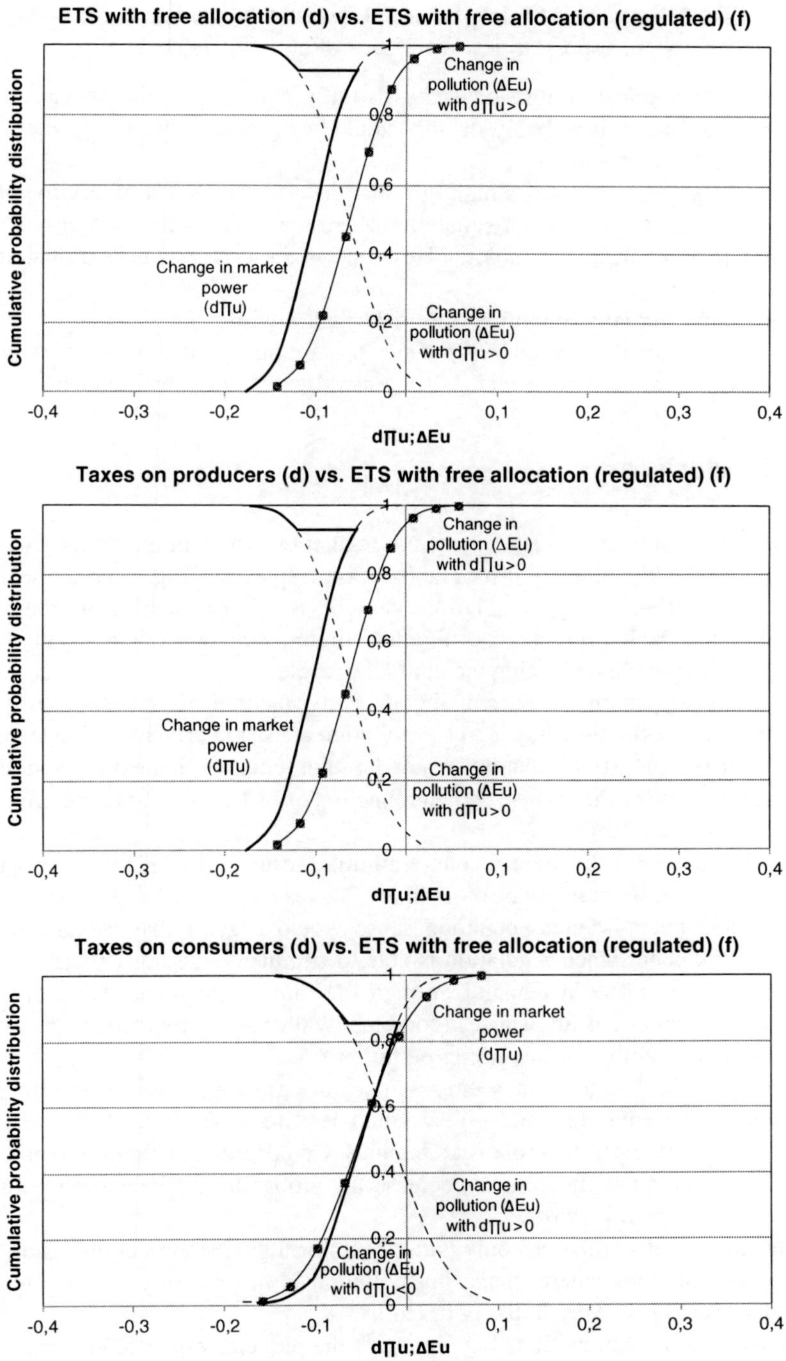

Fig. 2.6 Heat pump (*d*) vs. district heating (*f*) $(r_b > r_a)$

of emissions rates) and for low values of the cumulative distributions if $r_b > r_a$ (these values correspond to low difference of emissions rates).

Overall, numerical simulations only partially confirm the theoretical results. Increasing pollution is unlikely or very unlikely in several situations where it is theoretically admissible.

In addition, the simulations highlight that the perverse effect of environmental policy is admissible in several situations where the dominant technology is more polluting than the fringe technology. However, in these situations its probability is relatively restricted.

This only partially confirms the risk that environmental policies, within polarized situations due to energy policies promoting low polluting technologies, could have a dual perverse effect, as suggested by the theoretical model.

5 Conclusions

This chapter analyses how environmental regulation works in imperfectly competitive markets with dominant firm. The focus is on space heating, a service sector in which different technological solutions can coexist. Consequently, environmental regulation may be hybrid. In fact different environmental tools (alone or combined) can be applied to the coexisting technological cycles.

In line with part of the current literature, the theoretical analysis proves that environmental regulation may increase pollution at least in principle. However, this analysis also demonstrates that this result does not require either extreme curvature (sharp concavity) of the inverse demand function or sufficiently large (environmental) asymmetry of firms.

In addition, some apparently counterintuitive results arise. Firstly, under taxation the perverse effect might be more likely if taxes are charged to producers rather than to consumers whereas common sense would suggest that taxation should always work better when regulation is able to stimulate emissions abatement and not only the decrease in demand through the impact on prices. Secondly, free allocation of emissions allowances (combined with pricing regulation) drastically reduces the probability of increasing pollution.

Finally, hybrid regulation seems to play a significant role in affecting the probability that environmental policy could lead to a perverse effect (or could avoid it). Nevertheless, this role is ambiguous. Compared to symmetric regulation, hybrid regulation can increase or decrease the probability of increasing pollution depending on several factors.

The numerical simulations only partially confirm the theoretical results. In fact, in several situations where increasing pollution is theoretically admissible, it is virtually excluded or very unlikely in reality.

In addition, the simulations highlight that the perverse effect of environmental policy is admissible in several situations where the dominant technology is more polluting than the fringe technology. This result partially might confirm the risk of trade-off between environmental regulation and policies aimed at supporting cleaner technologies. In fact, when polarized configurations are due to energy policies promoting the deployment of cleaner technologies (fringe technology), environmental regulation can lead to a dual effect, at least in principle. It might increase the risk that the dominant firm prefers to undercut the cleaner technology rather than to accommodate its production, and, at the same time, leading to increasing rather than decreasing pollution. However, the numerical simulations also show that in these situations the probability of increasing pollution, although admissible, is relatively low. As a consequence the risk of the above-mentioned dual effect, in real terms, is modest.

Finally the analysis also shows that the perverse effect of environmental policy arises only for particular pollution price intervals, namely if the pollution price is sufficiently low, lower than that value involving a switch in cost-efficiency between the dominant firm and the fringe (provided that $r_b < r_a$). This result suggests that, in some sectors and in some conditions of market structures, when the environmental policy is too modest its effect might be not only insufficient to meet the environmental target but also perverse.

Appendix

Proof of Lemma 1

By facing the rival, the more efficient firm has two alternative strategies: (1) behaving as the residual supplier by pricing above the indifference price or (2) maximizing its own production by setting the price just below the indifference price.

Let π_1^d and π_2^d be the profits corresponding to the first and second strategies above, respectively. The profit the dominant firm earns by choosing the first strategy is

$$\pi_1^d = (p_r - MC_d)(Q(p_r) - \bar{q}_f) + \tau\,\Gamma \tag{2.11}$$

where

$$p_r = \arg\max_p\ (p - MC_d)(Q - \bar{q}_f) + \tau\,\Gamma \tag{2.12}$$

and Γ is the amount of allowances allocated free of charge where $\Gamma \neq 0$ only with benchmarking of emissions allowances.

If the leader chooses the second strategy, it earns

$$\pi_2^d = (p_{n_a} - MC_d)Q(p_{n_a}) + \tau\,\Gamma \tag{2.13}$$

Thus the leader will choose the second strategy if and only if $\pi_1^d < \pi_2^d$, i.e. from (2.11) and (2.13) if and only if

$$(p_{n_a} - MC_d) > \frac{p_r - MC_d}{Q(p_{n_a})}(Q(p_r) - \bar{q}_f)$$

Then, by reasoning at margin and because of environmental regulation implementation, the dominant firm will move from strategy (1) to strategy (2) (decreasing market power) if

$$\left(\frac{\partial p_{n_a}}{\partial \tau} - \frac{\partial MC_d}{\partial \tau}\right)Q(p_{n_a}) + (p_{n_a} - MC_d)\frac{\partial Q}{\partial p}\frac{\partial p_{n_a}}{\partial \tau} > \\ \left(\frac{\partial p_r}{\partial \tau} - \frac{\partial MC_d}{\partial \tau}\right)(Q(p_r) - \bar{q}_f) + \frac{\partial Q}{\partial p_r}\frac{\partial p_r}{\partial \tau}(p_r - MC_d) \tag{2.14}$$

and from strategy (1) to strategy (2), vice versa.

Since from (2.12)

$$\frac{\partial p_r}{\partial \tau}(Q(p_r) - \bar{q}_f) + \frac{\partial p_r}{\partial \tau}\frac{\partial Q}{\partial p}(p_r - MC_d) = 0$$

condition (2.14) becomes

$$d\Pi_u = \left(\frac{\partial p_{n_a}}{\partial \tau} - \frac{\partial MC_d}{\partial \tau}\right) - \frac{(Q(p_r) - \bar{q}_f)^2}{Q^2(p_{n_a})}\frac{\partial p_{n_a}}{\partial \tau} + \\ \frac{\partial MC_d}{\partial \tau}\frac{(Q(p_r) - \bar{q}_f)}{Q(p_{n_a})} > 0 \tag{2.15}$$

Inversely, if the leader will move from strategy (1) to strategy (2) (increasing market power).

It is to be noted that if the pollution price is very high such that the leader becomes the less efficient firm (so losing its cost and price leadership), after regulation the former leader always prefers to set its residual price since it can never undercut the rival. Therefore, demand and pollution will always decrease.

Proof of Corollary 1

If input taxes are applied to both dominant firm's and fringe's consumers then the residual demand curve will be:

$$QR = \left(Q(p_r) - \bar{q}_f + r_a\tau\frac{\partial Q}{\partial p}\right)$$

Equation (2.11) becomes:

$$\pi_1^d = (p_r - MC_d)\left(Q(p_r) - \bar{q}_f + r_a(0)\,\tau\frac{\partial Q}{\partial p}\right)$$

At the same time, (2.13) becomes:

$$\pi_2^d = (p_{n_a} - MC_d)\left(Q(p_{n_a}) + r_b(0)\tau\frac{\partial Q}{\partial p}\right)$$

By following the same procedure adopted in the proof of Lemma 1, condition (2.5) follows.

If input taxes are applied only to the dominant firm's consumers then the residual demand curve will be:

$$QR = \left(Q(p_r) - \bar{q}_f + r_a\tau\frac{\partial Q}{\partial p}\right)$$

Equation (2.11) becomes:

$$\pi_1^d = (p_r - MC_d)\left(Q(p_r) - \bar{q}_f + r_a(0)\,\tau\frac{\partial Q}{\partial p}\right)$$

At the same time the profit corresponding to the strategy 2 is:

$$\pi_2^d = (p_{n_a} - MC_d)Q(p_{n_a})$$

By following the same procedure adopted in the proof of Lemma 1, condition (2.6) follows.

References

Canton J, Saubeyran A, Stahn H (2008) Environmental taxation and vertical Cournot oligopolies: how eco-industries matter. Environ Resour Econ 40:369–382

Chernyavs'ka L, Gullì F (2008) Marginal CO_2 cost pass-through under imperfect competition. Ecol Econ 68:408–421

Chernyavs'ka, Gullì F (2009) Environmental taxation within electricity auctions with dominant firm. International Energy Workshop (IEW) proceeding 2009, Venice

Conrad K, Wang J (1993) The effect of emission taxes and abatement subsides on market structure. Int J Ind Organ 11:499–518

Gullì F (2008) Modeling the short-run impact of carbon emissions trading on the electricity sector. In: Gullì F (ed) Markets for carbon and power pricing in Europe: theoretical issues and empirical analyses. Edward Elgar, Aldershot, UK and Brookfield, WI

Levin D (1985) Taxation within Cournot oligopoly. J Public Econ 27:281–290

Requate T (2005) Environmental policy under imperfect competition – a survey. CAU, Economics Working Papers, no 2005–12

Sugeta H, Matsumoto S (2007) Upstream and downstream pollution taxations in vertically related markets with imperfect competition. Environ Resour Econ 38:407–432

Chapter 3
Pollution Under Environmental Regulation Within Multi-Period Auctions: The Case of Electricity Markets

Abstract This chapter aims at exploring how imperfect competition can affect the performance of environmental policy. The focus is on power generation which is a particularly interesting case for three reasons. First it is one of the most important environmentally regulated markets. Second the demand for electricity varies cyclically over time (for example on hourly basis). Third the pricing mechanism is a multi-period and multi-unit first price auction. The main finding of the analysis is that, looking at the entire demand cycle, it is very unlikely that imperfect competition may lessen the performance of environmental policy although, in line with the current literature, the analysis shows that pollution can increase within specific cycle periods, at least in the short-run.

1 Introduction

How can imperfect competition affect the performance of environmental policy? In this chapter we give an additional contribution on this issue relying on comparative statics and focusing on power generation which is a particularly interesting case for three reasons. First it is one of the most important environmentally regulated markets. Second the demand for electricity varies cyclically over time (for example on hourly basis). Third the pricing mechanism is a multi-period and multi-unit first price auction.

The analysis is a static analysis since we do not account for abatement and/or for how the environmental policy can impact on investments. However this may not be a severe limitation. In fact, the short-run impact is crucial for the long-run as far as what happens in the short-run makes it more or less difficult, and thus more or less expensive, to meet the long-run environmental targets. For instance, this may occur when the possible increase in pollution in the short-run implies the need for more investments in clean technologies in order to meet the long-run targets.

As pointed out in the introduction of this book (Chap. 1), several articles of the economic literature deal with environmental policy under imperfect competition.

F. Gullì, *Pollution Under Environmental Regulation in Energy Markets*,
Lecture Notes in Energy 6, DOI 10.1007/978-1-4471-4727-5_3,

They provide a controversial framework. Some authors (Levin 1985; Requate 2005) find that increasing pollution is admissible under specific conditions of supply and demand. Other authors show that environmental policy increases pollution never (Sugeta and Matsumoto 2007; Canton et al. 2008).

These contributions deal with general contexts where firms own a single technology and face a single demand curve. What does it happen when firms operate several technologies and plants (multi-unit and multi-technology supply) and face variable demand and consequently a set of demand function (multi-period supply). This is the typical case arising in electricity wholesale spot markets where firms compete within multi-period and multi-unit price auctions.

According to a part of the current literature, the analysis carried out in this chapter demonstrates that under imperfect competition environmental policy can in principle increase emissions within specific time periods. This may occur only under specific (and presumable unlikely) conditions. However it also emerges that, if we look at the entire demand cycle, increasing pollution is virtually impossible.

The chapter proceeds as follows. Section 2 focuses on the structure of the model used to characterize price equilibria under imperfect competition. Section 3 deals with how environmental policy can change the degree of market power. Section 4 focuses on how environmental regulation can impact on pollution. Finally, Sect. 5 summarizes the main findings of the analysis.

2 The Basic Model

2.1 Assumptions

First of all, it is important to describe the structure of the model detailing the main assumptions on the regulation of the output market.

We assume that the demand function can be represented by the load duration curve $D(p,H)$ where H is the number of periods (e.g., number of hours) in the reference time period (e.g., the day or the year) that demand is equal to or higher than D, with $0 \leq H \leq H_L$, and p is the spot price. $D_L(p) = D(p,H_L)$ is the minimum demand and $D_M(p) = D(p,0)$ is the maximum demand. Furthermore, for all (p,H), $-\infty < \partial D/\partial p < 0$ and $\partial D/\partial H < 0$. Given the load duration curve, the model will characterize equilibrium price for each level of demand of the load curve, that is $\forall H \in [0;H_L]$.

We assume linear technologies. The constant per-unit variable cost of production (essentially the fuel cost per unit of output) is $c \geq 0$. The constant emission rate (emissions per unit of output) is $r \geq 0$. Therefore pollution is proportional to output.

Without loss of generality, we restrict the analysis to two groups of technologies, a and b. Each of them includes a large number of homogeneous units such that

$$K_j = \sum_i k_j^i, \quad j = a,b \quad \text{and} \quad c_j^i = c_j;\ r_j^i = r_j,\ \forall i,j$$

where $c_j^i = c_j \geq 0$, $r_j^i = r_j \geq 0$, and $k_j^i = k_j > 0$ are the per-unit variable cost, the emission rate, and the capacity of the i-th unit belonging to the group j, respectively.

Thus K_a and K_b are the installed capacity of groups a and b, respectively, with $K_a + K_b = K_T = D_M$, i.e., the units of kind a and b are sufficient to meet the maximum demand. K^d and K^f are the installed capacity of the dominant firm and the fringe, respectively. $q^j \in [0, K^j]$, with $j = d,f$, is the amount of electricity produced in the generic hour by the firm j.

As pointed out before, in our model we consider homogeneous plants whose c_j and r_j do not depend on output. This assumption does not reflect the real conditions of operation for two reasons. First power generation costs include cycling costs[1] which vary with the level of demand. Second power stations may show different fuel costs even if they belong to the same group of technologies (using the same fuel). However we continue to assume constant variable costs and emission rates because this allows us to greatly simplify the analytical structure of the model without undermining its significance, as we will explain later when we will present and comment the results of the model.

We simulate two technological scenarios: (1) Scenario 1 where there is trade-off between variable costs and emission rates (hereafter "trade-off in the plant mix"), i.e., the technology with lower variable cost is the worse polluter ($c_a < c_b$ but $r_a > r_b$) and (2) Scenario 2 where there is not such a trade-off, i.e., the technology with lower variable cost is also the cleaner technology ($c_a < c_b$ and $r_a < r_b$).

Environmental regulation is based on pollution taxes (proportional to emissions) or on emissions trading (ETS). The pollution price, τ, is the charge per unit of pollutant emitted. This is well suited to describe the case of CO_2 emissions and therefore the case in which the pollution tax is a carbon tax and ETS is a carbon ETS.

Given this framework, the variable cost of the generating units belonging to the group j of plants includes the "pollution cost," $r_j \cdot \tau \cdot q_j$, where $q_j \in [0; k_j]$ is the amount of electricity produced in the generic hour. Therefore under either taxation or ETS, the marginal cost is

$$MC_j = c_j + e_j \cdot \tau \quad \text{with} \quad j = a, b \tag{3.1}$$

[1] The cycling cost is the additional cost of power generation when the generation unit is operating on margin that is when it meets varying demand and consequently has to adjust its output frequently, including frequent start-up and shut-down. The cost of cycling depends on the type of technology. Cycling involves increasing costs due to higher fuel costs and component degradation. The level of this additional cost depends on the type of technology. For example it is higher for coal plants than for gas plants. By using the analysis carried out by Denny and O'Malley (2009), it is possible to estimate the cycling costs of a system including coal and gas units in the same proportion (50 % coal and 50 % gas). Within this system, the unit cycling cost is about 6 and 10 Euro/MWh when the gas plants and the coal plants operate on the margin, respectively. This component is important if we want to account for the fact that the strategic behavior involves additional cost for power firms. In fact, the dominant firm could not follow a strategy in which it actually reduced output once the level of demand became high enough to support a supposed equilibrium at the maximum price. First, it is expensive to adjust the level of output from power stations, particularly if the required pattern would involve reducing output at first and then increasing it as demand rises further.

From (3.1) and for the purpose of this analysis, the units belonging to the group j of plants are defined as the more (less) efficient units if their marginal cost is lower (higher) than that of the units belonging to the other group i.

Furthermore, if $r_a > r_b$ there exists a pollution price, the "switching price," $\tau^s = (c_b - c_a)/(r_a - r_b)$, such that the marginal cost of the plants of the group a, MC_a, is equal to that of the plants of the group b, MC_b. Then $\overline{MC} = \max\{MC_a; MC_b\}$ is the marginal cost of the less efficient plants and $\underline{MC} = \min\{MC_a; MC_b\}$ the marginal cost of the more efficient ones.

To simulate market power we use a dominant firm facing a competitive fringe model.[2] This model is used in the literature concerning environmental policy under imperfect competition and it is well suited to simulate the structural features of several electricity markets.

The leader (d) and the competitive fringe (f) supply the market with capacity given by $K^d > 0$ and $K^f > 0$, respectively. The general formulation of the model assumes that the dominant firm and the fringe operate both kinds of plants, a and b.

With regard to the organization of the electricity market, we consider a typical spot market in which the pricing mechanism is a multi-period uniform first price auction.

Firms simultaneously submit bid prices for each of their units and for each period (each hour). The auctioneer collects and ranks the bids by applying the merit order rule. The bids are ordered by increasing bid prices and form the basis upon which a market supply curve is carried out.

If called upon to supply, firms are paid according to the market-clearing spot price (the system marginal price is equal to the highest bid price accepted). All players are assumed to be risk neutral and to act in order to maximize their expected payoff (profit). Production costs, emission rates as well as firms' installed capacity are common knowledge.

Furthermore, throughput the analysis we assume efficient rationing. This means that, when the dominant firm (holding the most efficient technology) and the fringe set the same prices (namely the marginal cost of the fringe), the most efficient firm serves the consumers first. However, as explained later, assuming proportional rationing does not change the overall results of the analysis.

Finally, we make the hypothesis that firms' offer prices are constrained below some threshold level, $\hat{p}$, which can be interpreted as follows.

[2] This model is used in the literature on the environmental policy under imperfect competition, see Conrad and Wang (1993), Bonacina and Gullì (2007), Chernyavs'ka and Gullì (2008), and Gullì (2008). On the methodological side, the attraction of this characterization is that it avoids the implausible extreme of perfect competition and pure monopoly, at the same time escaping the difficulties of characterizing an oligopolistic equilibrium. In particular, this model allows us to overcome the problem of possible inexistent equilibria in pure strategy. In their article on spot market competition in the UK electricity industry, using a typical duopolistic framework, von der Fehr and Harbord (1993) demonstrate that under variable-demands period (i.e., when the range of possible demands exceeds the capacity of the largest generator) there does not exists an equilibrium in pure strategy. Instead, there exists a unique mixed-strategy Nash equilibrium.

We can suppose that the threshold is not introduced officially but simply perceived by the generators (an implicit or informal price cap). For instance firms believe that the regulator will introduce (or change) price regulation if the price rises above a certain threshold. More likely, we assume that strategic firms, rather than to maximize profits, try to pursue a profit target, because of the regulatory pressure exerted by the competition and sector-specific authorities.

Given this assumption, it is reasonable to assume that the price cap is a function of either τ or H. It depends on pollution price because the dominant firm will try to pass-through to price threshold the increase in cost due to environmental regulation. It depends on H because it is likely that the mark-up coefficient could increase with the power demand and consequently could decrease with H. In fact, the dominant firm will try to apply higher mark-up in the hours of higher demand.[3]

Finally it is important to underline that, consistently with what really occurs in electricity markets, the model assumes that demand is sensitive to price but that price elasticity is low. Consequently, it is reasonable to assume that price threshold is always lower than the corresponding residual monopoly price. This is the implicit assumption adopted throughput the paper.

2.2 *Equilibria*

Given the regulatory framework described above, it is straightforward that power price equilibria will depend on power demand level. As the latter continuously varies over time, a useful way of representing the price schedule is carrying out the so-called price curve $p(H)$.

In order to derive the price schedule in the form of a price curve, we introduce the following parameters.

The first parameter is $\delta \in [0; 1]$ representing the share of total capacity in the market operated by the dominant firm.

Then the competitive fringe will operate a share $1 - \delta$ of total capacity and δ can be interpreted as a measure of degree of market concentration.

The other parameters are $\underline{\mu}^d \in [0; 1]$ and $\underline{\mu}^f \in [0; 1]$ representing the share of capacity the strategic operator and the competitive fringe hold in most efficient plants, respectively.

By complement, $\bar{\mu}^d = 1 - \underline{\mu}^d$ and $\bar{\mu}^f = 1 - \underline{\mu}^f$ are the same in the least efficient ones.

[3] However, this assumption is not crucial for the analysis. We introduce it in order to be closer to real operation of electricity markets. In these markets, in fact, prices generally do not jump suddenly above the marginal cost. The Lerner index grows smoothly with the ratio of demand to capacity (Borenstein et al. 2002; Wolfram 1998).

Let $\underline{K}^f$ be the installed capacity in most efficient plants operated by the competitive fringe. Thus $\underline{K}^f = \underline{\mu}^f(1-\delta)K_T$ and $\underline{H}^f = D^{-1}(\underline{K}^f)$.

Finally, $\underline{K} = \left[\underline{\mu}^d\delta + \underline{\mu}^f(1-\delta)\right]K_T$ is the total capacity in most efficient plants.

Facing the competitive fringe, the dominant firm maximizes its profit given the residual demand. Given that marginal costs are constant, this means that it has two alternative strategies:

1. Bidding the price threshold ($\hat{p}$) so accommodating the maximum production by the fringe or
2. Competing *à la Bertrand* with the rivals in order to maximize its market share.

The following Lemma describes the shape of the price curve.

Lemma 1. *(i) There exists* $\hat{D} \in \left[D_M, \underline{K}^f\right]$ *such that in any equilibrium (i)* $p = \hat{p}$ *if* $D \geq \hat{D}$, *(ii)* $p = \overline{MC}$ *if* $\underline{K}^f \leq D < \hat{D}$ *and (iii)* $p = \underline{MC}$ *if* $D < \underline{K}^f$, *where*

$$\hat{D} = \begin{cases} D_1 = \left[\underline{\mu}^d\delta\zeta + (1-\delta)\right]K_T & \text{if} \quad \hat{D} \geq \underline{K} \\ D_2 = (1-\delta)\left[\dfrac{1-\underline{\mu}^f\zeta}{1-\zeta}\right]K_T & \text{if} \quad \hat{D} < \underline{K}. \end{cases}$$

with $\zeta = \dfrac{\overline{MC} - \underline{MC}}{\hat{p} - \underline{MC}}$

Proof. See Appendix. Figure 3.1 illustrates the results of this lemma graphically for the case in which $\hat{D} = \hat{D}_1$.

Lemma 1 states that there is a demand threshold above which the dominant firm bids the price threshold and below which it prefers to bid prices just below the marginal cost of the fringe's generating units. Therefore $\hat{D}$ can be considered as a proxy of the degree of market power. In fact, $\hat{H} = D^{-1}(\hat{D})$ is the time (the number of hours) over which the dominant firm prefers to set the price threshold.[4]

On the basis of this interpretation, we assume that market power increases when the number of hours in which the dominant firm prefers to bid the price threshold goes up ($\hat{H}$ increases and $\hat{D}$ decreases). Instead there will be a decrease in market power, vice versa ($\hat{H}$ decreases and $\hat{D}$ increases).

To find empirical evidence helpful to support this result, we carried out the empirical analysis of the Italian power market in which Enel, the dominant firm, is able to exert a significant degree of market power. The Italian market can be divided

[4] Indeed, the dominant firm exerts its market power not only when it bids the residual monopoly price but also when it is able to set prices just below the marginal cost of the least efficient units, whereas under perfect competition prices would converge to the marginal cost of the most efficient ones. We ignore this "second effect" since it depends on $\underline{K}^f$ which does not depend on the tax rate.

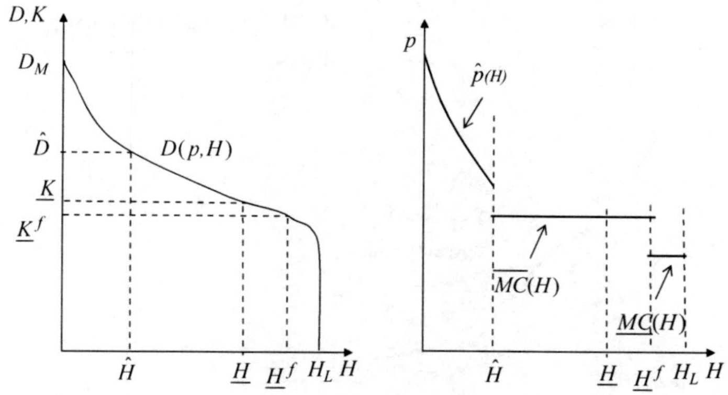

Fig. 3.1 The model output: load duration curve and corresponding price curve

into four macro sub-markets: North, South, Sardinia, and Sicily. The North sub-market is the largest of them and its structure significantly changed over time. In 2006 there was a relatively high degree of market power which almost disappeared in 2009.[5] This occurred without significant changes in the distribution over time (hour by hour) of the marginal technologies (technologies setting prices).

Therefore the comparison between the price curve for 2006 and the price curve for 2009, appropriately corrected in order to sterilize the difference of fuel costs (the dynamic of fuel prices), may provide a good representation of the difference between imperfect and full competition. The results of this comparison are illustrated in Fig. 3.2. They seem to support the prediction of the simulation model. Up to a certain level of power demand (corresponding to about 3,500–4,000 h), the two curves are almost identical. Above this level the 2006 curve (the imperfectly competitive one) increases much more than that for 2009 (the fully competitive one) as predicted by Lemma 1.[6]

Note that the price curve in Fig. 3.1 is a quasi-stepped curve, and not a quasi-continuous increasing curve (as in Fig. 3.2). This is because we do not account for cycling costs and because we consider homogeneous plants (within the same group of technologies). As pointed out before, this assumption is not realistic but it does not undermine the significance of our analysis for the following reason. Accounting for cycling costs and plants' non-homogeneity modifies $\underline{MC}$ and $\overline{MC}$ and consequently the value of ζ so changing just the value of $\hat{D}$ but not its structure (see Lemma 1).

---

[5] In order to check the incentive to use market power we can use the so-called Residual Supply Index (RSI).The RSI is equal to the sum of the overall quantities offered by sale minus the number of the operators multiplied by the difference between the sum of the overall quantities offered by sale and the sum of the overall quantities sold. Consequently, the higher the RSI, the more profitable is to behave as the residual supplier, i.e., the more profitable to behave strategically. The average hourly RSI was 2,825 in 2006 and 1,720 in 2009.

[6] Moreover, the empirical analysis of North of Italy sub-market also highlights that the coal plants, whose share of installed capacity is around 10 %, are the marginal units (i.e., units setting prices) in around 10 % of the peak hours. This is a signal that this technology can be (and indeed is) used for strategic behavior that is to exert market power.

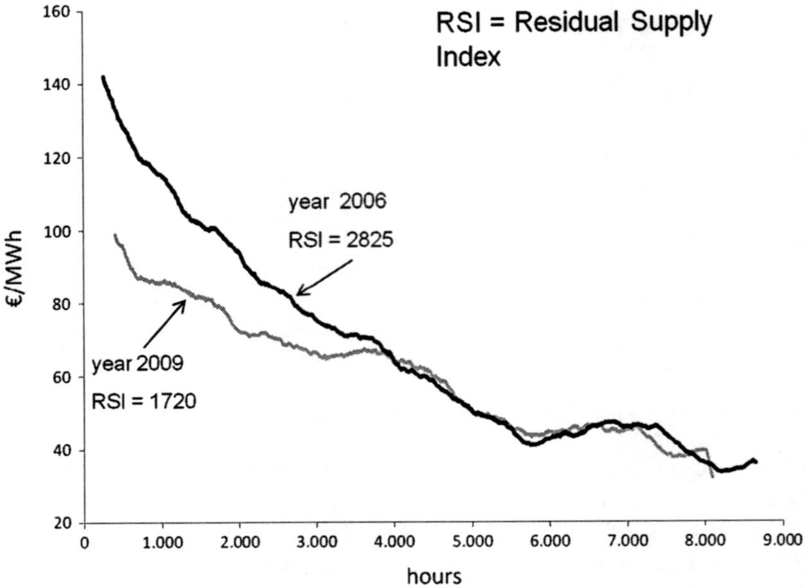

Fig. 3.2 Price curves in the Italian North sub-markets: 2006 (more market power) vs. 2009 (much less market power)

3 The Effect on Market Power

Lemma 1 also highlights that the degree of market power depends on the parameter ζ. Since this latter depends on pollution price, environmental regulation is able to modify the degree of market power. The following lemma describes how this can occur.

Lemma 2. $\partial\hat{D}/\partial\tau > 0$ *if* $\partial\hat{p}/\partial\tau < r_k + \dfrac{r_l - r_k}{c_l - c_k}(\hat{p}(0) - c_k)$ *and vice versa, with* $k = a$ *and* $l = b$ *when* $\tau < \tau^s$ *and* $k = b$ *and* $l = a$ *when* $\tau \geq \tau^s$.

Proof. For the formal proof, see Appendix. Intuitively, the environmental regulation can increase market power when the change in the cost structure between the technologies makes it more profitable bidding the price threshold rather than the marginal cost of the least efficient plants. This occurs when the proportional increase (decrease) in the difference between the price threshold and the marginal cost of the most efficient plants is higher (lower) than the proportional increase (decrease) in the difference between the marginal cost of the least efficient and the most efficient plants.

Lemma 2 also implies that the probability of increasing or decreasing market power depends on the price threshold sensitivity to the tax rate ($\partial\hat{p}/\partial\tau$).

Corollary 1. *If the dominant firm pursues a profit target ($\partial\hat{p}/\partial\tau > r_a$), (i) environmental regulation always increases market power ($\Delta\hat{D} < 0$) if $r_b < r_a$; (ii) if $r_b > r_a$ then $\Delta\hat{D} > 0$ when $(r_b - r_a)/(c_b - c_a)$ is sufficiently high; (iii) if $r_b < r_a$ and $\tau \geq \tau^s$ $\Delta\hat{D}$ may be either positive or negative.*

Proof. This corollary directly follows from Lemma 2 (see Appendix). Intuitively, if the dominant firm pursues a profit target, to keep constant the profit requires prices have to increase more than the increase in cost ($\Delta\hat{p} > r_a\tau$).

Finally, by differentiating $\hat{D}$ with respect to $\underline{\mu}^d$ and $\underline{\mu}^f$ we find that the degree of market power is an increasing function of $\underline{\mu}^f$ and a decreasing function of $\underline{\mu}^d$ (see Appendix).

Lemma 2 raises the following issues. First, under imperfect competition environmental regulation may lessen or amplify market distortions. Second (and most important), the change in market power due to environmental regulation might significantly impact on pollution as long as it can modify the production by the different groups of plants (the more and the less polluting plants). Thus the following questions arise. Can imperfect competition lessen the ability of environmental policy to reduce emissions or its ability to minimize the cost of meeting environmental targets? Can environmental policy determine a net rise (rather than a decrease) in pollution at least in the short-run? In the next section we will try to answer these questions.

4 The Effect on Pollution

In fully competitive markets environmental regulation can modify the amount of pollutant emissions by means of two effects. On the one hand, it determines a decline in pollution as long as it causes an increase in prices and consequently a decrease in demand (and production). On the other hand, if $r_b < r_a$ and if the pollution price is above the "switching tax," it determines a switch of producers on the merit order. This switch reduces significantly the production by the more polluting plants.

In imperfectly competitive markets, apart from these two possible effects, we have to take into account an additional one that is the just mentioned impact of pollution taxes on the degree of market power. This is due to the fact that, due to the implementation of environmental policy, the dominant firm changes its strategy in a certain number of hours. We denominate these hours as "on-change hours" while the remaining ones, in which the dominant firm's strategy remains unchanged, are denominated as "off-change hours."

Figure 3.3 illustrates how these hours are distributed when taxation determines a change in market power.

During the off-change hours, environmental regulation impacts on power demand only. In this case we have to distinguish two components (Fig. 3.3). The

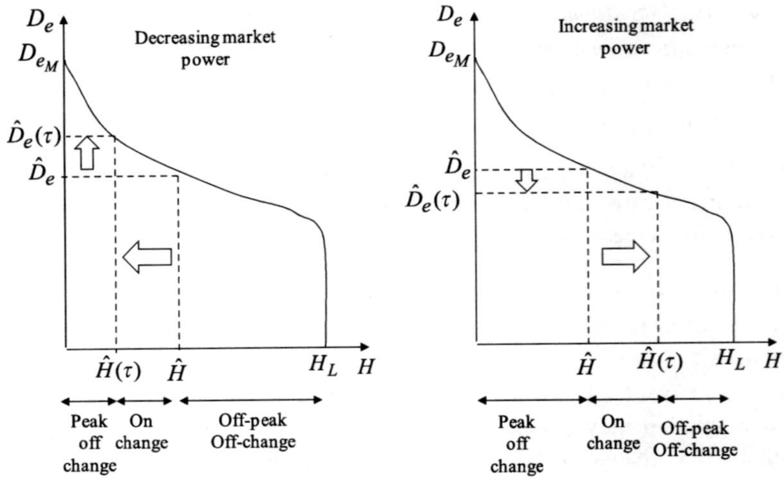

Fig. 3.3 Changes in market power in the load duration curve

first one is the change in emissions during the peak off-change hours. In these hours the dominant firm prefers to bid the price threshold before and after environmental policy. The second one is the change in emissions during the off-peak off-change hours in which the dominant firm prefers to bid the marginal cost of the less efficient units before and after the environmental regulation.

Instead, the change in emissions in the on-change hours is due to two combined sub-effects: (1) the (direct) effect (ΔE_{on}^{dir}) caused by the dominant firm's strategic decision in terms of production (restraining or maximizing production) and (2) the (indirect) effect (ΔE_{on}^{ind}) caused by the impact of the dominant firm's strategy on prices and consequently on demand and production.

For the sake of simplicity we refer to the basic case in which the dominant firm holds only one group of units (units a) and the fringe only the other one (units b) that is the case in which $\mu_a^d = 1$ and $\mu_a^f = 0$. The analysis of this specific case has two advantages. First it emphasizes the result of the model since, under these conditions, the change in emissions in the on-change hours is clearer. Second it allows us to greatly simplify the analytical explanation without loss of generality.

If $r_b < r_a$ and $\tau < \tau^s$ then $\Delta \hat{D} < 0$. In the on-change hours, before environmental regulation the dominant firm prefers to maximize its production (by units a, the more polluting ones) by bidding prices below the marginal cost of the fringe's plants (units b):

$$\begin{cases} q^d(0) = q_a(0) = K^d \\ q^f(0) = q_b(0) = D(c_b) - K^d \end{cases}$$

After regulation, the leader bids the price threshold by restraining its production (by units a) and accommodating the fringe's maximum production:

$$\begin{cases} q^d(\tau) = q_a = D(\hat{p}(\tau)) - K^f \\ q^f(\tau) = q_b = K^f \end{cases}$$

Therefore, since there is also a significant increase in price, the production by the more polluting plants, units a, sharply goes down and there will be a strong decrease in emissions ($\Delta E_{on}^{dir} < 0$ and $\Delta E_{on}^{ind} < 0$):

$$\Delta E_{on} = r_a D(\hat{p}(\tau)) - r_b D(c_b) + (r_b - r_a)(K^d + K^f) < 0$$

At the same time, prices sharply go up (and emissions go down) in the peak and off-peak on-change hours ($\Delta E_{off} < 0$). Consequently, the result is a net decrease in pollution ($\Delta E = \Delta E_{on} + \Delta E_{off} < 0$).

It is to be noted that when demand is less than the fringe's capacity (i.e., when the dominant firm and the fringe offer the same price, MC_b) only the dominant firm's units (the most polluting and most efficient plants) are despatched. This implicitly assumes the efficient rationing. However, with the proportional rationing and multi-unit auctions the result would remain substantially unchanged.[7] At the same time, when demand is above the fringe's total capacity the rationing rule is not relevant since the dominant firm always bids below or above the marginal cost of the fringe.

If $r_b > r_a$ then $\Delta\hat{D} < 0$ or $\Delta\hat{D} > 0$. If $\Delta\hat{D} < 0$ environmental policy determines a decrease in the production of the less polluting plants (units a) and an increase in production by the more polluting plants ($\Delta E_{on}^{dir} > 0$). Nevertheless prices go up and consequently total production and corresponding emissions decrease ($\Delta E_{on}^{ind} < 0$):

$$\Delta E_{on} = r_a D(\hat{p}(\tau)) - r_b D(c_b) + (r_b - r_a)(K^d + K^f)$$

The net result in the on-change hours is therefore ambiguous. Emissions can increase only if the difference in emission rates between technologies is very high (large environmental asymmetry of firms) but, in this case, $\Delta\hat{D} < 0$ is very unlikely (Corollary 1), unless $c_b - c_a$ is very high (large structural asymmetry of firms). In addition, in the off-change hours pollution certainly and sharply goes down. Therefore, looking at the entire demand cycle, increasing pollution is virtually impossible.

---

[7] With multi-unit auctions, strictly speaking, only offer prices of sets that may become marginal need equal the system marginal price. Thus proportional rationing has a negligible impact on pollution if the unit size is relatively small.

If $r_b > r_a$ and $\Delta\hat{D} > 0$, before environmental regulation:

$$\begin{cases} q^d(0) = q_a(0) = D(\hat{p}(0)) - K^f \\ q^f(0) = q_b(0) = K^f \end{cases}$$

After environmental regulation:

$$\begin{cases} q^d(\tau) = q_a(\tau) = K^d \\ q^f(\tau) = q_b(\tau) = D(MC_b) - K^d \end{cases}$$

The change in emissions is

$$\begin{aligned} \Delta E_{on} &= r_a[q_a(\tau) - q_a(0)] - r_b[q_b(\tau) - q_b(0)] = \\ &= r_b D(MC_b) - r_a D(\hat{p}(0)) + (r_a - r_b)(K^d + K^f) \end{aligned} \tag{3.2}$$

Environmental policy determines a decrease in the production of the more polluting plants (units b) and an increase in production by the less polluting plants ($\Delta E_{on}^{dir} < 0$). Nevertheless prices go down so that total production and corresponding emissions increase ($\Delta E_{on}^{ind} > 0$). Once again, the net result in the on-change hours is therefore ambiguous. But this time, emissions can increase only if the difference in emission rates between technologies is very low (low environmental asymmetry of firms).

However this makes it less likely that $\Delta\hat{D} > 0$ (the number of on-change hours becomes very restricted) unless $c_b - c_a$ is very low. In addition, once again, in the off-change hours pollution certainly and sharply goes down. Therefore, looking at the entire demand cycle, increasing pollution is very unlikely.

The above arguments can be summarized:

Proposition 1. *Within multi-periods electricity auctions, under imperfect competition it is very unlikely (virtually impossible) that environmental regulation could increase pollution.*

Proof. See Appendix (for the formal proof) and comments above.

5 Conclusions

In the introduction of this chapter, we raised the following question. How does imperfect competition affect the performance of environmental policy?

Focusing on power generation, one of the most important environmentally regulated markets, we find that, in line with a part of the current literature, imperfect competition may increase pollution (at least in principle) in the short-run and in specific time-periods, namely in the hours in which the dominant firm changes its strategy moving from the situation before to that after environmental regulation (the on-change hours). However this may happen only under specific and unlike conditions.

In addition, if we look at the entire demand cycle, including the hours in which the dominant firm does not change its strategy (the off-change hours), it emerges that absolute increasing pollution is virtually impossible. Emissions certainly decrease in the off-change hours while, as pointed out before, the increase in the on-change hours is unlikely.

Finally it is worth underlying that this analysis assumes that markets for power generation inputs are fully competitive and strategic firms, in output markets, pursue a (short-term) profit target. Further research work is needed in order to check what happens if also the input market (e.g., the natural gas market) is imperfectly competitive and if strategic firms maximize profit or pursue a long-term profit target. Imperfect competition also in the input market, in fact, may change the results making it more or less likely the conditions for the absolute increase in pollution in the short-run. This analysis will be carried out in the next chapter of the book.

Appendix

Proof of Lemma 1

Let $\bar{K} = D_M - \bar{K}^d$ be the peak demand minus the dominant firm's capacity in least efficient plants ($\bar{K}^d$) with $\bar{H} = D^{-1}(\bar{S})$. It is immediately intuitive that when $D \geq \bar{K}$ the system marginal price equals the price threshold, $\hat{p}$. When $D \leq \underline{K}^f$, pure Bertrand equilibria (first marginal cost pricing) arise and prices equal the marginal cost of the most efficient plants ($\underline{MC}$). In fact, on the one hand, whenever the demand is so high that both leader's and fringe's less efficient units can enter the market, the dominant firm would not gain any advantage by competing à la Bertrand, i.e., by attempting to undercut the rivals. Therefore, it will maximize its profit by bidding the price threshold. On the other hand, whenever the power demand is lower than the fringe's power capacity in most efficient plants, competing à la Bertrand is the only leader's available strategy in order to have a positive probability of entering the market. In consequence prices will converge to the marginal cost of the most efficient plants.

It remains to identify the leader's optimal choice[8] on $D \in \left]\overline{K}; \underline{K}^f\right]$. Under the assumptions of the model, each firm in the competitive fringe has a unique dominant strategy whatever is the market demand: bidding according to its own

[8] It is to be noted that assuming a dominant firm with competitive fringe model, rather than an oligopolistic framework, assures that equilibria in pure-strategy do exist. For an explanation of why equilibria in pure strategies do not exist in the case of oligopolistic competition, see von der Fehr and Harbord (1993, 1998).

marginal cost of production. By converse the best choice of the dominant firm might consist in (*i*) bidding the price threshold ($\hat{p}$) or in (*ii*) bidding $\overline{MC}$.

Let π_A^d and π_B^d be the profits corresponding to the first and second strategies above, respectively. Whenever the least efficient units could enter the market (i.e., $D \geq \underline{K}$), the profit the dominant firm earns by choosing the first strategy (i.e., $\forall H \in]\bar{H}; \underline{H}]$) is

$$\pi_A^d = (\hat{p} - \underline{MC})[D - (1 - \delta)K_T] \tag{3.3}$$

If the dominant firm chooses the second strategy, he earns

$$\pi_B^d = (\overline{MC} - \underline{MC})\delta\underline{\mu}^d K_T \tag{3.4}$$

Therefore the leader's optimal strategy is bidding the price threshold if and only if $\pi_A^d \geq \pi_B^d$, i.e., if and only if

$$D \geq D_1(\delta, \underline{\mu}^d, \zeta) = \left[\underline{\mu}^d \delta\zeta + (1 - \delta)\right] K_T \tag{3.5}$$

where

$$\zeta = \frac{\overline{MC} - \underline{MC}}{\hat{p} - \underline{MC}}$$

When $D \in \left]\underline{K}; \underline{K}^f\right]$ (i.e., $H \in \left]H; \underline{H}^f\right]$) the profit the dominant firm earns by choosing the first strategy is

$$\pi_C^d = (\hat{p} - \underline{MC})[D - (1 - \delta)K_T] \tag{3.6}$$

and by choosing the second strategy the profit is

$$\pi_D^d = (\overline{MC} - \underline{MC})\left[D - \underline{\mu}^f (1 - \delta)K_T\right] \tag{3.7}$$

Thus the dominant firm will choose the first strategy if and only if $\pi_C^d \geq \pi_D^d$, i.e., if and only if

$$D \geq D_2 = (1 - \delta)\left[\frac{1 - \zeta\underline{\mu}^f}{1 - \zeta}\right] K_T \tag{3.8}$$

Summarizing, the dominant firm will prefer to bid the price threshold when

$$D \geq \hat{D} = \begin{cases} D_1 = \left[\underline{\mu}^d \delta\zeta + (1-\delta)\right] K_T & \text{if} \quad \hat{D} \geq \underline{K} \\ D_2 = (1-\delta)\left[\dfrac{1-\underline{\mu}^f \zeta}{1-\zeta}\right] K_T & \text{if} \quad \hat{D} < \underline{K} \end{cases}$$

By differentiating $\hat{D}$ with respect to $\underline{\mu}^d$ and $\underline{\mu}^f$ we get

$$\frac{\partial D_1}{\partial \underline{\mu}^d} = K_T \delta\zeta > 0$$

and

$$\frac{\partial D_2}{\partial \underline{\mu}^f} = -K_T(1-\delta)\frac{\zeta}{1-\zeta} < 0$$

Proof of Lemma 2

The derivative of $\hat{D}$ with respect to τ can be written as

$$\frac{\partial \hat{D}}{\partial \tau} = \frac{\partial \hat{D}}{\partial \zeta}\frac{\partial \zeta}{\partial \tau} \tag{3.9}$$

From (3.5) and (3.8)

$$\frac{\partial D_1}{\partial \zeta} = \delta \underline{\mu}^d K_T > 0 \tag{3.10a}$$

and

$$\frac{\partial D_2}{\partial \zeta} = \frac{(1-\delta)(1-\underline{\mu}^f)}{(1-\zeta)^2} K_T > 0 \tag{3.10b}$$

Then the degree of market power is a decreasing function of ζ.
By differentiating ζ with respect to τ, we get

$$\frac{\partial \zeta}{\partial \tau} = \frac{(r_b - r_a)(\hat{p}(0) - c_b) - (\partial \hat{p}/\partial \tau - r_a)(c_b - c_a)}{(\hat{p} - c_a - r_a \tau)^2} \tag{3.11}$$

if $\tau < \tau^s$ and

$$\frac{\partial \zeta}{\partial \tau} = \frac{(r_a - r_b)(\hat{p}(0) - c_a) - (\partial \hat{p}/\partial \tau - r_b)(c_a - c_b)}{(\hat{p} - c_b - r_b \tau)^2} \tag{3.12}$$

if $\tau \geq \tau^s$.

Therefore $\partial\zeta/\partial\tau > 0$ and consequently $\partial \hat{D}/\partial\tau > 0$ if

$$\partial\hat{p}/\partial\tau < \hat{r} = r_k + \frac{r_l - r_k}{c_l - c_k}(\hat{p}(0) - c_k)$$

and vice versa, with $k = a$ and $l = b$ when $\tau < \tau^s$ and $k = b$ and $l = a$ when $\tau \geq \tau^s$.

Proof of Corollary 1

When $D \in \left]\overline{K}; \underline{K}^f\right]$ the profit that the dominant firm earns by setting the price threshold before environmental regulation is

$$\hat{\pi}^d(0) = (\hat{p}(0) - c_a)RD(\hat{p}(0)) \tag{3.13}$$

with $RD = D - K^f$.

After regulation the profit is

$$\hat{\pi}^d(\tau) = (\hat{p}(\tau) - MC_a)RD(\hat{p}(\tau)) \tag{3.14}$$

Then, $\hat{\pi}^d(\tau) = \hat{\pi}^d(0)$ implies that

$$(\hat{p}(\tau) - c_a) = (\hat{p}(0) - c_a)\frac{RD(\hat{p}(0))}{RD(\hat{p}(\tau))} + \tau \cdot r_a \tag{3.15}$$

Then from (3.15) it follows that

$$(\hat{p}(\tau) - \hat{p}(0)) > r_a \cdot \tau.$$

Furthermore, from (3.11):

When $r_b < r_a$ and $\tau < \tau^s$ then $\dfrac{\partial\zeta}{\partial\tau} > 0$ and consequently $\dfrac{\partial \hat{D}}{\partial\tau} > 0$ if

$$\partial\hat{p}/\partial\tau < \hat{r} = r_a + \frac{r_b - r_a}{c_b - c_a}(\hat{p}(0) - c_a)$$

and vice versa. Therefore if $\partial \hat{p}/\partial\tau > r_a$ then $\dfrac{\partial \hat{D}}{\partial\tau} < 0$ always.

When $r_b > r_a$, $\dfrac{\partial\zeta}{\partial\tau} > 0$ and consequently $\dfrac{\partial \hat{D}}{\partial\tau} > 0$ if

$$\partial\hat{p}/\partial\tau < \hat{r} = r_a + \frac{r_b - r_a}{c_b - c_a}(\hat{p}(0) - c_a)$$

and vice versa. Therefore if $\partial\hat{p}/\partial\tau > r_a$ then $\frac{\partial\hat{D}}{\partial\tau}$ may be either positive or negative depending on $(r_b - r_a)/(c_b - c_a)$.

From (3.12):

When $r_b < r_a$ and $\tau \geq \tau^s$, the condition

$$\partial\hat{p}/\partial\tau < \hat{r} = r_b + \frac{r_a - r_b}{c_a - c_b}(\hat{p}(0) - c_b)$$

is always satisfied. Consequently $\frac{\partial\zeta}{\partial\tau} > 0$ and $\frac{\partial\hat{D}}{\partial\tau} > 0$ always.

Finally, it is to be noted that when $\tau \geq \tau^s$ we should look at the discrete variation of $\hat{D}$ ($\Delta\hat{D}$) that is at the variation from zero to $\tau \geq \tau^s$. In this case $\Delta\hat{D}$ may be either positive or negative regardless of the first derivative $\partial\hat{D}/\partial\tau$.

In fact, from (3.5) we get $\hat{D}(\tau = 0) > \hat{D}(\tau > \tau^s)$ if

$$\mu_a^d > \mu_b^d \frac{\hat{p} - c_a}{(\hat{p} - c_b - r_b\tau)(c_b - c_a)}[c_a - c_b + \tau(r_a - r_b)] \tag{3.16}$$

This means that $\Delta\hat{D}$ may be either positive or negative depending on μ_a^d, μ_b^d, and τ. The higher the μ_a^d and the lower the μ_b^d and τ the more likely that $\Delta\hat{D} < 0$. Vice versa for $\Delta\hat{D} > 0$.

Proof of Lemma 3 and Proposition 1

Assume for example the supply configuration described in Fig. 3.4 (case of $\hat{D} \geq \underline{K}$; $\tau < \tau^s$ and $r_b < r_a$). Given the price curve described in Proposition 1, the total amount of pollutant emissions, E, is

$$\begin{aligned} E = {} & r_b\left[\int_0^{\bar{H}(p(\tau))} D(H,p(\tau))dH - (K_a^d + K_a^f)\bar{H}\right] + r_a(K_a^d + K_a^f)\bar{H} + \\ & + r_a\left[\int_{\bar{H}(p(\tau))}^{\hat{H}(p(\tau))} D(H,p(\tau))dH - K_b^f(\hat{H} - \bar{H})\right] + r_b K_b^f(\hat{H} - \bar{H}) + \\ & + r_b\left[\int_{\hat{H}(p(\tau))}^{\underline{H}(p(\tau))} D(H,p(\tau))dH - (K_a^d + K_a^f)(\underline{H} - \hat{H})\right] + \\ & + \; r_a(K_a^d + K_a^f)(\underline{H} - \hat{H}) + r_a\left[\int_{\underline{H}(p(\tau))}^{H_L} D(H,p(\tau))dH\right] \end{aligned} \tag{3.17}$$

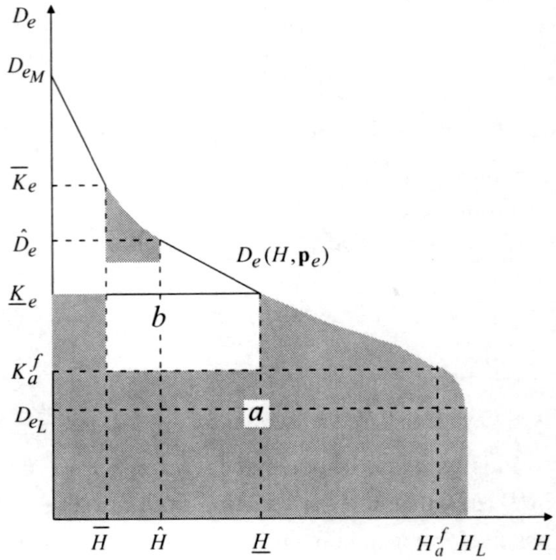

Fig. 3.4 Example of supply configuration: production by units of group *a* (*grey area*); production by units of group *b* (*white area*)

By differentiating (3.17) with respect to τ and given that

$$\frac{\partial}{\partial \tau}\left[\int_{H_i(p(\tau))}^{H_j(p(\tau))} D(H,p(\tau))dH\right] = D(H_j,p(\tau))\frac{\partial H_j}{\partial \tau} - D(H_i,p(\tau))\frac{\partial H_i}{\partial \tau} + \\ + \int_{H_i(p(\tau))}^{H_j(p(\tau))} \frac{\partial D(H,p(\tau))}{\partial \tau} dH$$

we get

$$\frac{\partial E}{\partial \tau} = (r_b - r_a)(\overline{K} - \hat{D})\frac{\partial \hat{H}}{\partial \tau} + r_b\left[\int_0^{\overline{H}(p(\tau))} \frac{\partial D(H,p(\tau))}{\partial \tau} dH\right] + \\ + r_a\left[\int_{\overline{H}(p(\tau))}^{\hat{H}(p(\tau))} \frac{\partial D(H,p(\tau))}{\partial \tau} dH\right] + r_b\left[\int_{\hat{H}(p(\tau))}^{\underline{H}(p(\tau))} \frac{\partial D(H,p(\tau))}{\partial \tau} dH\right] + \\ + r_a\left[\int_{\underline{H}(p(\tau))}^{H_L} \frac{\partial D(H,p(\tau))}{\partial \tau} dH\right] \tag{3.18}$$

The first element on the right side of (3.18) is the change in emissions in the on-change hours caused by the change in market power (excluded the effect due to the change in demand), ΔE_{on}^{dir}. This effect is due to the modification in the share of production by the different technology groups. We denominate this component as

$$A = (r_b - r_a)(\overline{K} - \hat{D})\frac{\partial \hat{H}}{\partial \tau}$$

Therefore, since $\hat{D} \leq \overline{K}$, $A > 0$ $(A < 0)$ if $r_b < r_a$ and $\frac{\partial \hat{H}}{\partial \tau} < 0$ $\left(\frac{\partial \hat{H}}{\partial \tau} > 0\right)$. Vice versa if $r_b > r_a$.

The remaining elements in (3.18), the integrals, represent the change in emissions due to demand effect caused by the change in prices. We denominate the sum of these four elements as B.

Provided that the discrete change in emissions due to the pollution price τ is given by

$$\Delta E = \int_0^{\tau} \frac{\partial E}{\partial \tau} d\tau = \int_0^{\tau} A d\tau + \int_0^{\tau} B d\tau, \quad \forall \tau \in [0; \hat{\tau}] \tag{3.19}$$

the environmental policy will increase pollution $(\Delta E > 0)$ only if

$$C = \int_0^{\tau} A d\tau > F = -\int_0^{\tau} B d\tau, \quad \forall \tau \in [0; \hat{\tau}] \tag{3.20}$$

where $\hat{\tau}$ is the tax rate above which the demand effect (the decrease in demand) is so high that aggregate emissions necessarily go down regardless of the market power effect.

Then we may have the following situations corresponding to the possible combinations (Table 3.1) of pollution price (τ), sensitivity of the power price threshold $(\partial \hat{p}/\partial \tau)$ and change in market power.

1. Configuration (AII). In this case, since $\frac{\partial \hat{H}}{\partial \tau} > 0, \forall \tau$ and $r_b < r_a$. Then $C < 0$, on the one hand. On the other hand, the increase in market power determines an increase in price and consequently a decrease in emissions due to the decrease in demand (amplified by the rise in the price threshold even if low). Therefore $F > 0$, $C < F$, and consequently $\Delta E < 0$ [from (3.18) and (3.19)].
2. Configurations (BI). In these cases $\frac{\partial \hat{H}}{\partial \tau} < 0, \forall \tau$ and $r_b > r_a$. Then $C < 0$, on the one hand. On the other hand, the decrease in market power determines a drop in prices and consequently an increase in emissions due to the increase in demand in the on-change hours. This increase is partially or totally offset by the decrease in emissions in the off-change periods. Therefore the result is ambiguous but it is likely that $F > 0$ and consequently $\Delta E < 0$.
3. Configuration (BII): This time $\frac{\partial \hat{H}}{\partial \tau} > 0$, $\forall \tau$ and $r_b > r_a$. Therefore, on the one hand $C > 0$. On the other hand, the increase in market power determines a rise in

Table 3.1 Change in emissions

	$\tau < \tau^s$		$\tau \geq \tau^s$	
	$\partial\hat{p}/\partial\tau < \hat{r}$	$\partial\hat{p}/\partial\tau > \hat{r}$	$\partial\hat{p}/\partial\tau < \hat{r}$	$\partial\hat{p}/\partial\tau > \hat{r}$
	I	II	III	IV
(A) $r_b < r_a$				
$\partial\hat{p}/\partial\tau > r_a$		$\Delta\hat{D} < 0$	$\Delta\hat{D} > 0; \Delta\hat{D} < 0;$	$\Delta\hat{D} > 0; \Delta\hat{D} < 0;$
		$(\Delta E < 0)$	$(\Delta E < 0)$	$(\Delta E < 0)$
(B) $r_b > r_a$				
$\partial\hat{p}/\partial\tau > r_a$	$\Delta\hat{D} > 0$	$\Delta\hat{D} < 0$		
	$(\Delta E < 0; \Delta E > 0^{(*)})$	$(\Delta E < 0; \Delta E > 0^{(*)})$		

(*) Very unlikely

prices and consequently a decrease in emissions in the on-change hours. This rise is largely amplified by the decrease in emissions in the off-change hours also because the price cap is highly sensitive to pollution price. This means that the result is ambiguous in principle but it is very likely that $F > 0$, $C < F$, and consequently $\Delta E < 0$.

4. Configurations (AIII) and (AIV). In these cases, as pointed out before (Proof of Corollary 1), we have to look at the discrete variation of $\hat{D}$ ($\Delta\hat{D}$) which may be either positive or negative. Consequently $\Delta\hat{H}$ may be either negative or positive, respectively. However, it is possible to demonstrate that $A < 0$ and $C < 0$ in both cases. If $\Delta\hat{D} < 0$ the increase in market power implies the increase in the share of production by the least polluting plants, then $A < 0$. In addition, prices increase and emissions decrease everywhere, then $B < 0$ and $F > 0$. Consequently $C < F$ and $\Delta E < 0$. If $\Delta\hat{D} > 0$ the decrease in market power determines the increase in the share of production by the least polluting plants, then $A < 0$ and $C < 0$ again. Furthermore, prices decrease during the on-change hours but this decrease (and its effect on emissions) is totally or partially offset by the increase in prices (and consequently by the corresponding fall in demand and production) during the off-change hours. Thus once again it is very likely that $C < F$ and consequently that $\Delta E < 0$ [from (3.18) and (3.19)].

Finally, it is possible to demonstrate that these results arise even for the case in which $\hat{D} \leq \underline{K}$.

References

Bonacina M, Gullì F (2007) Electricity pricing under "carbon emission trading": a dominant firm with competitive fringe model. Energy Policy 35:4200–4220

Borenstein S, Bushnell J, Wolak F (2002) Measuring market inefficiencies in California's restructured wholesale electricity market. Am Econ Rev 92(5):1376–1405

Canton J, Saubeyran A, Stahn H (2008) Environmental taxation and vertical Cournot oligopolies: how eco-industries matter. Environ Resour Econ 40:369–382

Chernyavs'ka L, Gullì F (2008) Marginal CO_2 cost pass-through under imperfect competition. Ecol Econ 68:408–421

Conrad K, Wang J (1993) The effect of emission taxes and abatement subsides on market structure. Int J Ind Organ 11:499–518

Denny E, O'Malley M (2009) The impact of carbon prices on generation-cycling costs. Energy Policy 37:1204–1212

Gullì F (2008) Modeling the short-run impact of carbon emissions trading on the electricity sector. In: Gullì F (ed) Markets for carbon and power pricing in Europe: theoretical issues and empirical analyses. Edward Elgar, Aldershot, UK and Brookfield, WI

Levin D (1985) Taxation within Cournot oligopoly. J Public Econ 27:281–290

Requate T (2005) Environmental policy under imperfect competition – a survey. CAU, Economics Working Papers, no 2005–12

Sugeta H, Matsumoto S (2007) Upstream and downstream pollution taxations in vertically related markets with imperfect competition. Environ Resour Econ 38:407–432

von der Fehr N, Harbord D (1993) Spot market competition in the UK electricity industry. Econ J 103(418):531–546

von der Fehr N, Harbord D (1998) Competition in electricity spot markets – economic theory and international experience, Memorandum, n. 5, Department of Economics, University of Oslo

Wolfram CD (1998) Strategic bidding in a multiunit auction: an empirical analysis of bids to supply electricity in England and Wales. RAND J Econ 29(4):703–725

Chapter 4
Pollution Under Imperfect Competition in Vertical Related Energy Markets

Abstract This chapter aims at identifying the mechanisms through which imperfect competition in energy markets can affect the performance of environmental policy. Vertical related markets are investigated: (1) the electricity market (output market); (2) the market for natural gas (input market). Two supply scenarios are simulated: (1) Scenario 1 (highly polluting supply) where power generation is based on more polluting technologies; (2) Scenario 2 (cleaner supply) where power generation is based on cleaner technologies. Finally, two regulatory scenarios are explored: (a) Scenario A where firms can maximize profits; (b) Scenario B when, because of the regulatory pressure exerted by competition and sector-specific authorities, firms pursue strategies besides the profit maximization, namely by pursuing a short- or long-term profit target. The analysis shows that imperfect competition may lessen the performance of environmental policy, that is its ability to reduce pollution and/or its ability to minimize the cost of meeting environmental targets, in either Scenario 1 or Scenario 2 and in either Scenario A or Scenario B. However, in Scenario 2 relatively low pollution prices are necessary. Furthermore, this effect seems to be more likely when firms can maximize profits (Scenario A) rather than under regulatory pressure (Scenario B) unless environmental regulation is based on ETS with benchmarking and firms pursue a long-term profit target. Finally, looking at the entire demand cycle, increasing pollution in the short run is virtually excluded or very unlikely in all cases.

1 Introduction

This chapter aims at further deepening the analyses carried in the previous chapters. The performance of environmental policy is evaluated by considering imperfect competition in two vertical related energy markets, namely:

1. The electricity market (output market), which constitutes one of the most important markets subjected to environmental regulation (e.g., power generation is the largest sector covered by the European Emissions Trading Scheme, the EU ETS).

F. Gullì, *Pollution Under Environmental Regulation in Energy Markets*, Lecture Notes in Energy 6, DOI 10.1007/978-1-4471-4727-5_4,

2. The natural gas markets (input market), which represents one of the basic inputs for power generation in several countries.

Two supply scenarios are simulated: (1) Scenario 1 (highly polluting supply) where power generation is based on more polluting technologies; (2) Scenario 2 (cleaner supply) where power supply is based on cleaner technologies.

The analysis is a comparative static analysis. Emissions abatement and/or the impact on investments are not accounted for and so is the change in market structure. Consequently, if we observe the entire compliance period, the results may be interpreted as the expression of what can happen in the short run. Note that this does not constitute a limitation of the analysis. As observed in Chap. 1, short-run impact is crucial for the long-run one, as the former can make it more difficult (and expensive) to meet long-term targets.

Similarly to previously analyzed cases, environmental regulation is based on pollution taxes or on emissions trading (ETS). In case of taxation, the level of emissions is the dependent variable. Consequently, increased pollution in the short run might undermine the possibility of meeting the expected environmental target. In case of ETS, the emissions target is exogenous (independent variable). This implies that ETS is surely able to meet the expected emissions reduction (at least in principle). However, increased pollution in the short run can make it more difficult to reduce emissions. This undermines the performance of ETS, namely its ability to minimize the cost of meeting the environmental target. We deduce this ability through the short run or, its equivalent, the inertial change in emissions. It is proven that, if the short run or inertial decrease in emissions under imperfect competition is lower than under full competition, or even more if there is an absolute increase in pollution, a greater effort of abatement is needed, with the following policy implication. If models used to simulate the performance of environmental regulation assume full competition in energy markets, they can overestimate environmental policy performance. Consequently, this may lead to the acceptance of more severe environmental targets or to underestimate the cost associated to meeting a specific target.

Furthermore, the analysis aims at studying how environmental policy interacts with competition policy whose impact is simulated, in this chapter, by considering two regulatory scenarios: (a) Scenario A, when firms can maximize profits (in the absence of regulatory pressure); (b) Scenario B when, because of the regulatory pressure exerted by competition and sector-specific authorities, firms pursue strategies besides the profit maximization,[1] namely by pursuing a short- or long-term profit target.

As underlined in the introductory chapter, the analysis does not attempt to measure the overall change in social welfare. This measurement may be misleading, since it requires estimating the economic value of environmental damage which is largely uncertain. In this chapter, a mere sensitivity analysis is carried out in order to evaluate

[1] For an analysis of the carbon cost pass-through when firms maximize market shares or sales revenues, see Vivid Economics (2007) and Sijm et al. (2008a, b).

how imperfect competition can affect the performance of environmental policy and how competition policies can interact with environmental regulation.

In this regard, the main finding is that increasing pollution is virtually excluded or very unlikely in all cases.

However, imperfect competition may lessen the performance of environmental policy. This would be likely to occur in both supply scenarios and in both regulatory scenarios. Nevertheless, in Scenario 2 (cleaner supply) it is admissible only if pollution prices are relatively low whereas it seems to be more likely when firms can maximize profits rather than under regulatory pressure unless firms pursue long-term profit targets and environmental regulation is based on ETS with benchmarking.

Finally it is worth pointing out that the analysis does not claim to provide the best simulation of energy markets as it is based on a series of assumptions (about technologies, market structure, firms' behavior, etc.) that largely simplify the real operational conditions in these markets. However, these assumptions can make it easier to identify the mechanisms through which public action interacts with the structure of energy markets. The basic hypotheses, aimed at checking the robustness of results, will be discussed at the end of the chapter.

This chapter is organized as follows. Section 2 focuses on the model structure used to characterize equilibria under imperfect competition. Section 3 deals with the impact of environmental regulation on gas prices and on marginal costs of power technologies. Section 4 investigates how environmental policy can change the degree of market power in electricity markets, distinguishing the cases without and with regulatory pressure. Section 5 focuses on how the change in costs is passed through to electricity prices and on the consequent impact on pollution. Section 6 discusses the robustness of the results. Finally, Sect. 7 summarizes the analysis of main findings.

2 The Basic Model: Assumptions

This section describes the model structure by detailing the main assumptions on environmental regulation and the main hypotheses on the regulation of the electricity and gas markets.

2.1 The Environmental Regulation

The assumptions about the environmental regulation are quite simple. As previously pointed out, the environmental policy is based on taxes or on emissions trading (ETS).

ETS gives rise to a market for emissions allowances. This market is very large and it involves a large number of polluting firms so that none of them is able to exercise market power.

Permits are auctioned and/or benchmarked. The benchmark is the emission rate, r_{bn}, of the best power plant belonging to the groups of assumed technologies in the electricity market (even if not operating). This framework is consistent with the European carbon market created through the implementation of the EU ETS (European Union Emissions Trading Scheme).

Taxation is proportional to emissions (emissions taxes). The pollution price, τ, is equal to the tax rate which is the charge per unit of pollutant emitted. Therefore, it is exogenous by definition.

Finally, emissions abatement in the electricity sector is not possible or, equivalently, the abatement cost is infinitely costly. Therefore, the analysis proposed in this chapter is a short-run analysis.

2.2 The Natural Gas Market

The natural gas demand function, $D_g(p_g)$, is continuous and for all gas prices, p_g, $-\infty < \partial D_g / \partial p_g < 0$ and $\partial^2 D_g / \partial p_g^2 < 0$.

To simulate market power we adopt a dominant firm with competitive fringe model. This model is well suited to simulate the structural features of several natural gas markets.

The dominant firm (d_g) and the fringe (f_g) supply the market with capacity (e.g., supply capacity in cubic meters per day or per annum) given by $K_g^{d_g} > 0$ and $K_g^{f_g} > 0$, respectively, with $K_g^{d_g} > K_g^{f_g}$. The model assumes linear technologies whose cost per unit of gas delivered, $c_g \geq 0$, is constant. $c_g^{d_g}$ and $c_g^{f_g}$ are the leader's and fringe's costs, respectively, with $c_g^{d_g} < c_g^{f_g}$.

It is assumed that firms are price setting and all players are risk neutral. They act in order to maximize their expected payoff (profit). Production costs as well as firms' installed capacity are of common knowledge.

Natural gas firms serve several consumption segments (industry, power generation, residential sector, etc.). Consequently, even if large, firms operating in each segment (including power firms) are not able to exert significant market power on natural gas market.[2]

Natural gas trading is regulated by long-term contracts. These contracts include rules for price indexation over time. Therefore, they are consistent with the short-run horizon of the analysis.

The leader's production capacity is very large such that the dominant firm is able to serve the entire market by itself, i.e., $K_g^{d_g} \geq D_g(c_g^{d_g})$.

[2] This is a reasonable assumption. In addition, it allows us to avoid the problem of price indeterminacy due to the existence of bilateral market power.

Furthermore, natural gas has perfect substitutes, alternative fuels (AF), in each segment of consumption. Firms delivering alternative fuel are homogenous.

2.3 The Power Market

In power sectors the demand function can be represented by the load duration curve $D_e(p_e, H)$ where H is the number of hours in the referenced time period (e.g., day or year) that demand is equal to or higher than D_e, with $0 \leq H \leq H_L$, and p_e is the spot price. $D_{e_L}(p_e) = D(p_e, H_L)$ and $D_{e_M}(p_e) = D(p_e, 0)$ are the minimum and maximum demand, respectively. Demand is deterministic and for each hour is a linear downward sloping demand, $D_e(p_e) = \gamma - \beta \cdot p_e$ with $\beta > 0$.

Similarly to the gas case, to simulate market power the dominant firm with competitive fringe model is used (this choice is discussed in Sect. 6.3). This model is well suited to simulate the structural features of several electricity markets.

The dominant firm (d_e) and the fringe (f_e) supply the market with capacity (installed power in MW) given by $K^{d_e} > 0$ and $K^{f_e} > 0$, respectively. Once again, the model assumes (this assumption is discussed in Sect. 6.2.) linear technologies which are characterized by constant per-unit variable cost of production, $c_e \geq 0$, and by constant emission rate, $r \geq 0$ (emissions per unit of output, e.g., tCO_2/MWh). The fringe and the dominant firm supply the quantities $q_e^{f_e} \in \left[0; K_e^{f_e}\right]$ and $q_e^{d_e} \in \left[0; K_e^{d_e}\right]$, respectively.

Without loss of generality, we restrict the analysis to two groups of power technologies, group a and group g (gas-fired units), respectively. Each of them includes a large number n of homogeneous units such that

$$K_{e_j} = \sum\nolimits_{i=1,2,..n} k^i_{e_j},\ j = a, g \quad \text{and} \quad c^i_{e_j} = c_{e_j};\ r^i_j = r_j,\ \forall i, j$$

where $c^i_{e_j} = c_{e_j} \geq 0, r^i_j = r_j \geq 0$ and $k^i_{e_j} = k_{e_j} > 0$ are the variable cost, the emission rate and the capacity of the i-th unit belonging to the group j, respectively.

Thus, K_{e_a} and K_{e_g} are the installed capacity of groups a and g, respectively, with $K_{e_a} + K_{e_g} = K_{e_T} = D_{e_M}$, that is the units of kind a and g are sufficient to meet the maximum demand. $q_{e_a} \in [0; K_{e_a}]$ and $q_{e_g} \in \left[0; K_{e_g}\right]$ are the amounts of electricity produced by the groups a and g, respectively.

Furthermore, there is trade-off between variable costs and emission rates, namely technology with lower variable cost is the worse polluter ($c_{e_a} < c_{e_g}$ but $r_a > r_g$) and vice versa. This condition is well suited to simulate a very common technological configuration, specifically one that includes CCGT (Combined Cycle Gas Turbine) plants (group g) and plants more polluting than CCGT (group a), e.g., conventional coal power plants in Scenario 1. Finally, the main alternative to natural gas is a technology (see Sect. 2.2.) whose emissions rate is lower than the emissions rate of plants a, that is $r_{AF} < r_a$.

The marginal cost of the i-th unit belonging to group j of units is given by the first derivative of the total cost and, resulting from the assumptions described earlier, is

$$MC_{e_j} = c_{e_j} + r_j \cdot \tau, \quad \text{with} \quad j = a, g, AF \tag{4.1}$$

From (4.1) and for the purpose of this analysis, units belonging to group j of units are referred to as the most (least) efficient units if their marginal cost is lower (higher) than that of those units belonging to the other group.

Furthermore, there is a pollution price, called "switching price," $\tau^s = (c_{e_g} - c_{e_a})/(r_a - r_g)$, such that the marginal cost of the units of group a, MC_{e_a}, is equal to that of the units of group g, MC_{e_g}. $\overline{MC}_e = \max\{MC_{e_a}; MC_{e_g}\}$ is the marginal cost of the least efficient units and $\underline{MC}_e = \min\{MC_{e_a}; MC_{e_g}\}$ the marginal cost of the most efficient ones.

With regards to the organization of electricity market, we consider a typical spot market in which the pricing mechanism is a multishot uniform price auction. Firms simultaneously submit bid prices for each of their units and for each hour (short-lived auctions). The auctioneer collects and ranks the bids by applying the merit order rule. The bids are ordered by increasing bid prices and form the basis upon which a market supply curve is carried out. If suppliers submit different bids, lower bidding supplier's capacity is dispatched first. If this capacity is not sufficient to satisfy total demand, the higher bidding supplier's capacity is then dispatched to serve the residual demand, i.e., total demand minus the capacity of the lower bidding supplier. Considering the given assumptions about electricity demand and market structure, there is a unique price p_e^r which maximizes the dominant firms' profits from serving the residual demand, i.e., $p_e^r = \arg\max_{p_e} \{p_e [D_e(p_e) - K^{f_e}] - C_{e_d}\}$ where C_{e_d} is the dominant firm's total cost. p_e^r will be referred to as "residual monopoly price" (Fabra et al. 2002).

If called upon to supply, firms are paid according to the market-clearing spot price (equal to the highest bid price accepted). All players are assumed to be risk neutral and to act in order to maximize their expected payoff (profit). Production costs, emission rates as well as firms' installed capacity are common knowledge.

3 Change in Gas Prices and Change in Marginal Costs of Power Generation

In the dominant firm model the gas leader maximizes its profit on the residual demand. If we consider constant marginal costs, it is implied that the dominant firm faces two strategies: (1) to accommodate the fringe's maximum production by setting prices equal to the residual monopoly price; (2) to set prices equal to the marginal cost of the fringe, so as to maximize its own production. If we consider what really happens in several gas markets, the former strategy is far more likely.

Nevertheless, the leader may not be able to set residual monopoly price, because there is an alternative fuel that might be able to create a sort of price cap in the input market. In fact under the assumptions reported in Sect. 2.2 and if residual monopoly price is sufficiently high, the leader firm will set prices just below $\hat{p}_g$. This is the price which would make the end user indifferent when choosing between an installation using gas and the alternative technology.

This means that, in order to set $\hat{p}_g$, gas firms look at the long-run marginal cost of alternative fuel ($LRMC_{AF}$), which is the cost to deliver an additional unit of this output under the assumption that this requires investment in capacity expansion.[3] Then the price threshold, $\hat{p}_g$, will be equal to the long-run marginal cost of the alternative fuel power installation minus the extra fuel costs[4] of the gas-fired installation. This difference is the net long-run marginal cost ($NLRMC_{AF}$).

It is to be noted that this kind of pricing is also denominated as "market value principle." It is widely used for price indexation in natural gas long-term contracts.

Given this framework, the following Lemma characterizes price equilibria in the natural gas market with dominant firm and inter-fuel competition.

Lemma 1. *If the gas leader behaves as a residual monopolist and if residual monopoly price is high enough, in any equilibrium natural gas price is equal to the net long-run marginal cost of alternative fuel.*

Proof. See Fig. 4.1. Given natural gas demand, D_g, and fringe's maximum production, $K_g^{f_g}$, the residual demand will be RD_g. The residual demand curve has been constructed by using the efficient rationing rule. If the size of the fringe is enough low and the potential capacity of alternative fuel is low enough (namely higher than the dominant firm's residual demand at $\hat{p}_g$), the dominant firm will set the price threshold $\hat{p}_g$ if this is lower than the residual monopoly price. For a discussion about equilibria in duopolistic contexts, see Sect. 6.3.

Lemma 1 suggests that, in order to know the impact of environmental policy on natural gas prices, it is necessary to study how the implementation of environmental policy modifies $\hat{p}_g$.

Under taxation the outcome is immediate. From Lemma 1 and (4.1), the natural gas price threshold will be given by

$$p_g = \hat{p}_g = NRLMC_{AF} = \eta_g \left[c_{AF} + EXF_{AF} - EXF_g + \tau (r_{AF} - r_g) \right] \tag{4.2}$$

[3] In particular, in the model carried out in this chapter the long-run marginal cost of the alternative technology is represented by the average cost of the best alternative technology.

[4] Extra fuel costs include capital costs, operating and maintenance costs.

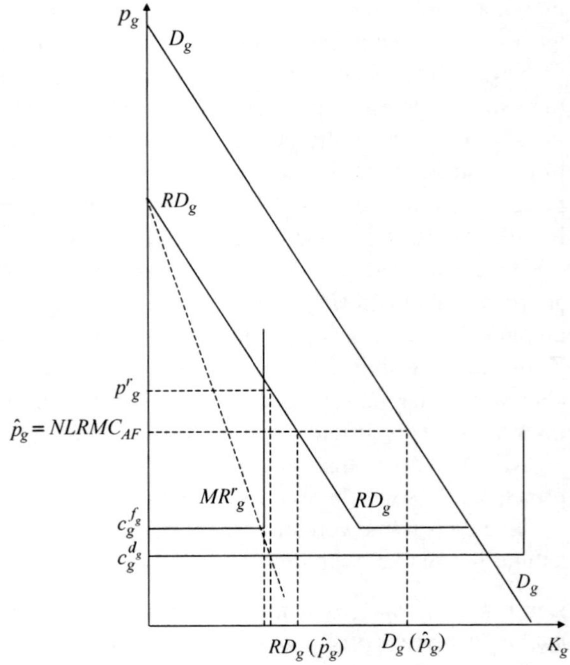

Fig. 4.1 Equilibrium in the natural gas market with inter-fuel competition (leader behaving as a residual monopolist)

where:

c_{AF} = fuel cost per unit of electricity generated by using alternative fuel installation;

EXF_j = extra fuel cost per unit of electricity generated, with $j = AF, g$;

η_g = electric efficiency of gas-fired power installation.

By differentiating (4.2) with respect to τ and provided that $p_g = \eta_g c_{e_g}$:

$$\left(\frac{dp_g}{d\tau}\right)_{tax} = \eta_g \frac{dc_{e_g}}{d\tau} = \eta_g (r_{AF} - r_g) \tag{4.3}$$

Equation (4.3) underlines an interesting result. If $r_{AF} > r_g$ ($r_{AF} < r_g$) taxation would determine an increase (a decrease) in gas price (and consequently in the fuel cost of gas-fired installations).

Under emissions trading the outcome depends on the method and on the rules of allowances allocation. To understand why and how, it is important to consider the following.

Firstly, ETS gives rise to a market for emissions allowances. Therefore, since allowances have a value their use generates an opportunity cost equal to the allowance price multiplied by the emission rate, $r_j\tau$, hereafter denominated as "pollution cost."

Secondly, as in case of taxation, ETS determines an increase in the unit variable cost equal to the pollution cost.

Thirdly, this cost arises even if public authority allocates to generators an amount of allowances free of charge. Nevertheless, the value of these allowances is a sort of "gift" for generators. Consequently, in order to calculate the net long-run marginal cost (which includes fixed components), the unit value of these allowances (value per unit of electricity generated) should be deducted from the cost. Then from Lemma 1 and (4.1), the natural gas price will be given by

$$\begin{aligned} p_g &= \hat{p}_g = NRLMC_{AF} = \\ &= \eta_g \left[c_{AF} + EXF_{AF} - EXF_g + \tau(E_{AF} - \bar{E}_{AF}) - \tau(E_g - \bar{E}_g) \right] \end{aligned} \tag{4.2bis}$$

where:

$E_j = r_j =$ actual emissions per unit of electricity generated, with $j = AF, g$;

$\overline{E}_j = r_{bn} =$ "emissions allocated" free of charge per unit of electricity generated, with $j = AF, g$;

With full auctioning, $\overline{E}_j = 0$. With benchmarking, $\overline{E}_j = r_{bn}$.

By differentiating (4.2bis) with respect to τ and provided that $p_g = \eta_g c_{e_g}$:

$$\left(\frac{dp_g}{d\tau}\right)_{ETS} = \eta_g \frac{dc_{e_g}}{d\tau} = \eta_g (r_{AF} - r_g) \tag{4.3bis}$$

Equations (4.3) and (4.3bis) point out two interesting results. Firstly, the change in price under ETS is equal to that under taxation. Secondly, in case of ETS, change in the gas price does not depend on the type of allowances allocation (auctioning or benchmarking[5]). These results are summarized in the following Proposition and Corollary.

Proposition 1. *In presence of imperfect competition in input (natural gas) market, the pollution price becomes a direct driver of the natural gas price.*

Proof. This Proposition is a direct consequence of Lemma 1.

Corollary 1. *The change in gas price due to environmental regulation depends on the difference in pollution costs between alternative fuel and natural gas fired power installations. In case of ETS, this result arises regardless of how allowances are allocated (auctioned or benchmarked).*

Proof. See (4.3) and (4.3bis) and above related comments.

In conclusion, imperfect competition gives rise to a direct link between natural gas prices and pollution prices as environmental policy directly impacts on natural gas prices through the cost of the alternative fuel. This impact (Table 4.1) depends on the type of alternative fuel.

In particular, it is important to underline that change in natural gas value is negative if the emission rate of the alternative fuel is lower than that of the gas-fired

[5] The result may be different under other types of free allocation (see Sect. 6.4).

Table 4.1 Impact of emissions trading on the input price

	Input market fully competitive	Input market imperfectly competitive
	Taxes, ETS with auctioning or benchmarking	
Gas price sensitivity	$\frac{dp_g}{d\tau} = 0$	$\frac{dp_g}{d\tau} = \eta_g(r_{AF} - r_g)$
Total change in marginal cost of gas fired technologies	$\Delta MC_{e_g} = r_g \cdot \tau$	$\Delta MC_{e_g} = r_{AF} \cdot \tau$

power station. This means that if alternative technology is a low carbon or carbon free technology (e.g., renewable technology or fossil fuels with Carbon Capture and Sequestration (CCS)) the environmental regulation determines a decrease in natural gas price. Otherwise there will be an increase.

From (4.1) it is implied that the marginal cost of the gas-fired plants will be equal to the fuel cost plus the alternative fuel carbon cost rather than that of the gas-fired one. In fact, for a generic $\tau > 0$:

$$MC_{e_g}(\tau) = c_{e_g}(\tau) + r_g \cdot \tau = c_{e_g}(0) + (r_{AF} - r_g) \cdot \tau + r_g \cdot \tau =$$
$$= c_{e_g}(0) + r_{AF} \cdot \tau \tag{4.4}$$

Consequently,

$$\Delta MC_{e_g}(\tau) = MC_{e_g}(\tau) - c_{e_g}(0) = r_{AF} \cdot \tau$$

Corollary 2. *Under imperfect competition in the gas market, the change in marginal cost of the gas-fired power units due to environmental regulation equals the alternative technology carbon cost.*

Proof. See (4.4) and Table 4.1.

4 Change of Market Power in Electricity Market

Given the assumptions on the power market described in Sect. 2.3, it is evident that power price equilibria will depend on power demand level. As the latter continuously varies over time, a useful way of representing the price schedule is to carry out the so-called price curve $p_e(H)$ by characterizing price equilibrium for every level of power demand in the load duration curve, i.e., for every value of H.

In order to derive the price schedule in the form of a price curve, it is useful to introduce the following parameters.

The first parameter is $\delta \in [0; 1]$ representing the share of the total capacity in the market operated by the leader. Then the fringe will operate a share $1 - \delta$ of the total capacity and δ can be interpreted as a measure of the degree of market concentration.

The other parameters are $\underline{\mu}^{d_e} \in [0;1]$ and $\underline{\mu}^{f_e} \in [0;1]$ representing the share of capacity both the leader and the fringe get in most efficient plants, respectively. By complement, $\bar{\mu}^{d_e} = 1 - \underline{\mu}^{d_e}$ and $\bar{\mu}^{f_e} = 1 - \underline{\mu}^{f_e}$ are the same in the least efficient ones.

By facing the fringe, the dominant firm will maximize the profit on the residual demand. Given that marginal costs are constant, this implies two possible strategies: (1) accommodating the maximum production by the fringe by bidding prices above the fringe's marginal cost or (2) competing *à la Bertrand* with the rivals in order to maximize its own market share.

Let $\underline{K}_e^{f_e}$ be the installed capacity in most efficient plants operated by the fringe. Thus, $\underline{K}_e^{f_e} = \underline{\mu}^{f_e}(1-\delta)K_{e_T}$ and $\underline{H}^f = D^{-1}(\underline{K}^{f_e})$. Finally, $\underline{K}_e = \left[\underline{\mu}^{d_e}\delta + \underline{\mu}^{f_e}(1-\delta)\right]K_{e_T}$ is the total capacity in most efficient plants.

4.1 Without Regulatory Pressure

The following Lemma describes the price curve shape when the dominant firm maximizes the profit.

Lemma 2. *(i) There exists $\hat{D}_e \in \left[D_{e_M}; \underline{K}_e^{f_e}\right]$ such that (i) $p_e = p_e^r$ if $D_e \geq \hat{D}_e$, (ii) $p_e = \overline{MC}_e$ if $\underline{K}_e^{f_e} \leq D_e < \hat{D}_e$ and (iii) $p_e = \underline{MC}_e$ if $D_e < \underline{K}_e^{f_e}$, where*

$$\hat{D}_e = \begin{cases} \hat{D}_{e_1} = \left[\underline{\mu}^{d_e}\delta\zeta + (1-\delta)\right] K_{e_T} & \text{if} \quad D_e \geq \underline{K}_e \\ \hat{D}_{e_2} = (1-\delta)\left[\dfrac{1-\zeta\underline{\mu}^{f_e}}{1-\zeta}\right] K_{e_T} & \text{if} \quad D_e < \underline{K}_e. \end{cases}$$

where $\zeta = \dfrac{\overline{MC}_e - \underline{MC}_e}{p_e^r - \underline{MC}_e}$

and $p_e^r = \arg\max_{p_e}\left\{p_e\left[D_e(p_e) - K^{f_e}\right] - C_{e_d}\right\}$

Proof. See Appendix.

$\hat{D}_e$ is a proxy of the degree of market power. In fact, $\hat{H} = D^{-1}(\hat{D}_e)$ is the time (number of hours) over which the dominant firm sets p_e^r.[6]

Lemma 2 highlights that two price curves are possible depending on whether the discontinuity is at $\hat{H}_1 = D^{-1}(\hat{D}_{e_1})$ or $\hat{H}_2 = D^{-1}(\hat{D}_{e_2})$.

---

[6] Indeed, the dominant firm exerts his market power not only when it bids the residual monopoly price but also when it is able to set prices just below the marginal cost of the least efficient units, whereas under perfect competition prices would converge to the marginal cost of the most efficient ones. We ignore this "second effect" since it depends on $\underline{K}_e^{f_e}$ which does not depend on the pollution price.

Finally, the degree of market power is an increasing function of $\underline{\mu}^{f_e}$ and a decreasing function of $\underline{\mu}^{d_e}$ (see Appendix).

Lemma 2 also shows that the degree of market power depends on ζ. Since the latter depends on pollution price, the environmental regulation is able to modify the degree of market power. Increasing market power means that the number of hours in which the dominant firm prefers to offer the residual monopoly price goes up. The opposite happens with decreasing market power. The following Lemma explains when this can occur.

Lemma 3. *If the dominant firm can maximize profits, environmental policy determines:*

(i) A decrease in degree of market power, $\Delta\hat{D}_e > 0$, in electricity market if

$$\bar{r} > \hat{r} = \underline{r}\left(1 - \frac{1}{2}\frac{D_e - (1-\delta)K_{e_T}}{K_a^d}\right)$$

where $\bar{r} = r_{AF}$ and $\underline{r} = r_a$ if $\tau < \tau^s$ while $\bar{r} = r_a$ and $\underline{r} = r_{AF}$ if $\tau \geq \tau^s$;

(ii) Vice versa (an increase in market power) if $\bar{r} < \hat{r}$;

(iii) When $\tau \geq \tau^s$ market power can either increase, $\Delta\hat{D}_e < 0$, or decrease, $\Delta\hat{D}_e > 0$.

Proof. See Appendix.

It is to be noted that the condition for change in market power in Lemma 3 is quite different than the same condition for the case of space heating described in Chap. 1. It is more restrictive for decreasing market power and less restrictive for increasing market power. This is because in electricity markets firms face a set of demand curves rather than a single demand curve.

Then in Chap. 1 the condition for change in market power is the condition under which the profit corresponding to the strategy 1 becomes higher than that related to the Strategy 2 (or vice versa), given the demand curve.

Here the condition for change in market power is slightly different. It is the condition under which to keep the equilibrium between the two strategies requires shifting from a demand curve to another.

This implies that, after the implementation of environmental regulation, searching for the condition for change in market power does not imply finding $\hat{r}$ (the value of $\bar{r}$ which makes the dominant firm indifferent when choosing between accommodating the fringe's production or maximizing its own production), given the demand curve. It implies finding the combination of $\hat{r}$ and demand curve which makes the dominant firm indifferent when choosing between these two strategies. If the new demand curve (after the environmental policy implementation) is above the former curve (before the environmental policy) there will be a decrease in market power and $\hat{r}$ will be higher than that value involving the change in strategy when the demand curve cannot change. Inversely, if the new demand curve is below the former curve, there will be an increase in market power. $\hat{r}$ will be lower than that value involving the change in strategy along the former demand curve.

4.2 With Regulatory Pressure

The basic model makes the assumption that firms can maximize profits, namely that the dominant firm can set the residual monopoly price.

However, firms may pursue strategies besides profit maximization. In particular, because of the regulatory pressure exerted by the competition and sector-specific authorities, their offer prices may be constrained to be below some threshold.

In other words, firms may restrain themselves to bid above some price threshold in order to avoid the risk of more restrictive regulation (implicit price cap).

In the presence of a price threshold, Lemma 2 becomes

Lemma 2bis. *(i) There exists* $\hat{D}_e \in \left[D_{e_M}; \underline{K}_e^{f_e}\right]$ *such that (i)* $p_e = \hat{p}_e$ *if* $D_e \geq \hat{D}_e$*, (ii)* $p_e = \overline{MC}_e$ *if* $\underline{K}_e^{f_e} \leq D_e < \hat{D}_e$ *and (iii)* $p_e = \underline{MC}_e$ *if* $D_e < \underline{K}_e^{f_e}$*, where*

$$\hat{D}_e = \begin{cases} \hat{D}_{e_1} = \left[\underline{\mu}^{d_e}\delta\,\sigma + (1-\delta)\right]K_{e_T} & \text{if} \quad D_e \geq \underline{K}_e \\ \hat{D}_{e_2} = (1-\delta)\left[\dfrac{1-\sigma\underline{\mu}^{f_e}}{1-\sigma}\right]K_{e_T} & \text{if} \quad D_e < \underline{K}_e. \end{cases}$$

where $\sigma = \dfrac{\overline{MC}_e - \underline{MC}_e}{\hat{p}_e - \underline{MC}_e}$

Proof. See Appendix.

Given this lemma the conditions under which environmental policy can increase or decrease market power become:

Lemma 3bis. *(i) When* $\tau < \tau^s$ *then* $\partial\hat{D}_e/\partial\tau \leq 0$ *if* $\partial\hat{p}_e/\partial\tau \geq \hat{r} = r_a + \lambda(r_{AF} - r_a)$ *and vice versa; (ii) When* $\tau \geq \tau^s$ *then* $\partial\hat{D}_e/\partial\tau \leq 0$ *if* $\partial\hat{p}_e/\partial\tau \leq \hat{r}$ *and vice versa, with* $\lambda = (\hat{p}_e(0) - c_{e_a})/(c_{e_g}(0) - c_{e_a}) > 1$

Proof. See Appendix.

Lemma 3bis underlines that, if the price threshold is sufficiently low sensitive to pollution price, environmental policy can decrease market power.

A typical case in which, because of regulatory pressure, firms offer below the profit-maximizing price is when they try to meet a short-term (e.g., one-period) or a long-term profit target (e.g., multiperiod target). This latter consists of keeping constant the profit over time, while at the same time minimizing price volatility.

The following Corollary describes the change in cost pass-through to price threshold under these different solutions.

Corollary 3. *Under imperfect competition, when the dominant firm bids the price threshold: (i) if the dominant firm pursues a short-term profit target, the pass-through rate may be less than one only with ETS and benchmarking of emissions allowances; (ii) if the dominant firm pursues a long-term profit target the pass-through rate may be much less than one only under ETS regardless of the kind of allowances allocation (auctioning or benchmarking).*

Table 4.2 Pollution cost pass-through with profit target

	Input market fully competitive	Input market imperfectly competitive		
		Pollution taxes	ETS with auctioning	ETS with benchmarking
Gas price sensitivity	$\frac{dp_g}{d\tau} = 0$		$\frac{dp_g}{d\tau} = \eta_g(r_{AF} - r_g)$	
$\hat{r}\ (\tau < \tau^s)$	$\hat{r} = r_a + \lambda(r_g - r_a)$		$\hat{r} = r_a + \lambda(r_{AF} - r_a)$	
Short-term target		$\frac{\partial \hat{p}_e}{\partial \tau} > r_a$	$\frac{\partial \hat{p}_e}{\partial \tau} > r_a$	$\frac{\partial \hat{p}_e}{\partial \tau} > r_a - r_{bn}$
Long-term target			$\frac{\partial \hat{p}_e}{\partial \tau} > \frac{1}{2} r_a$	$\frac{\partial \hat{p}_e}{\partial \tau} > \frac{1}{2} r_a - r_{bn}$

Proof. See Appendix.

Intuitively, if the profit target is a short-term target (e.g., one-period target), to keep the profit constant requires that prices have to increase more than the increase in cost, $\frac{\partial \hat{p}_e}{\partial \tau} > r_a$, because the price threshold is lower than the residual monopoly price (Table 4.2). If the profit target is long term the dominant firm can choose the following strategy: to pass-through less than the increase in cost, when the cost goes up; to pass-through less than the decrease in cost, when the cost goes down. The loss of profit in the former case (increasing cost) is offset by the additional profit in the latter case (decreasing cost). Consequently, the profit over time remains unchanged. Obviously, this can happen only under ETS. In case of taxation the pollution price is given exogenously and cannot change over time.

Looking at the long-term target and ETS, a last question remains: which change in prices (pass-through) will the dominant firm choose when the price goes up? It presumably will choose a value enough low to minimize the regulatory risk and simultaneously enough high to reduce the uncertainty effect about the time evolution of pollution prices. In fact a too low bid is risky when it is not possible to know in advance whether, when and how much the pollution price will decrease in the future.

Given these constraints, the most likely pass-through should be that expected by the regulator, namely a value equal or lower than the change in marginal cost of the marginal technology if the market was fully competitive.

Nevertheless, it is possible to demonstrate (see Appendix) that the increase in price cannot be lower than a specific value.

In fact, as explained previously, if the profit target is a long-term one, the dominant firm can choose to pass-through less than the increase in cost when the cost goes up (period $t = 1$), provided that the pass-through is sufficiently lower than the decrease in cost when the cost goes down (period $t = 2$).

The loss of profit in the former case is offset by the additional profit in the latter case. As a result, the average profit remains unchanged over time.

However this behavior is sustainable if (in case of a rise in pollution price) $\left(\frac{\partial \hat{p}_e}{\partial \tau}\right)_{t=1} > \frac{1}{2} r_a$ under auctioning and if $\left(\frac{\partial \hat{p}_e}{\partial \tau}\right)_{t=1} > \frac{1}{2} r_a - r_{bn}$ under benchmarking (Table 4.2).

It is to be noted that (see Appendix), when costs go down, the price drop is lower than the price increase when costs go up, in absolute terms. This is a typical behavior in those markets with market power and regulatory pressure.

Then given Lemma 3bis and Corollary 3:

Corollary 4. *Under regulatory pressure, if* $\tau < \tau^s$ *and if the dominant firm pursues a short-term profit target, environmental policy determines a decrease in degree of market power,* $\Delta \hat{D}_e > 0$, *in electricity market:*

(i) Under taxation or ETS with auctioning when

$$r_{AF} > \hat{r} = r_a \left[1 + (\rho - 1) \frac{D_e - (1-\delta)K_{e_T}}{K_a^d} \right]$$

with $\rho > 1$;

(ii) Under ETS with benchmarking when

$$r_{AF} > \hat{r} = r_a \left[1 + (\rho - 1) \frac{D_e - (1-\delta)K_{e_T}}{K_a^d} \right] - \rho \, r_{bn} \frac{D_e - (1-\delta)K_{e_T}}{K_a^d}$$

Proof. See Appendix.

Corollary 5. *Under regulatory pressure,* $\tau < \tau^s$ *and if the dominant firm pursues a long-term profit target environmental policy determines a decrease in degree of market power,* $\Delta \hat{D}_e > 0$, *in electricity market:*

(i) Under ETS with auctioning when

$$r_{AF} > \hat{r} = r_a \left[1 + \left(\frac{\rho}{2} - 1 \right) \frac{D_e - (1-\delta)K_{e_T}}{K_a^d} \right]$$

with $\rho > 1$;

(ii) Under ETS with benchmarking when

$$r_{AF} > \hat{r} = r_a \left[1 + \left(\frac{\rho}{2} - 1 \right) \frac{D_e - (1-\delta)K_{e_T}}{K_a^d} \right] - \rho \, r_{bn} \frac{D_e - (1-\delta)K_{e_T}}{K_a^d}$$

Proof. See Appendix.

4.3 Overall Framework

Table 4.3 summarizes the results described in the previous subsections. It reports the condition for decreasing market power (which is the most relevant issue).

Table 4.3 Conditions for decreasing market power ($\tau < \tau^s$)

	Input and output market imperfectly competitive		
	Pollution taxes	ETS with auctioning(*)	ETS with benchmarking(*)
Profit maximization		$r_{AF} > \hat{r} = r_a \left[1 - \frac{1}{2}\frac{D_e - K^f}{K_a^d}\right]$	
Short-term profit target	$r_{AF} > \hat{r} = r_a \left[1 + (\rho - 1)\frac{D_e - K^f}{K_a^d}\right]$	$r_{AF} > \hat{r} = r_a \left[1 + (\rho - 1)\frac{D_e - K^f}{K_a^d}\right]$	$r_{AF} > \hat{r} = r_a \left[1 + (\rho - 1)\frac{D_e - K^f}{K_a^d}\right] - \rho\, r_{bn}\frac{D_e - K^f}{K_a^d}$
Long-term profit target		$r_{AF} > \hat{r} = r_a \left[1 + \left(\frac{\rho}{2} - 1\right)\frac{D_e - K^f}{K_a^d}\right]$	$r_{AF} > \hat{r} = r_a \left[1 + \left(\frac{\rho}{2} - 1\right)\frac{D_e - K^f}{K_a^d}\right] - \rho\, r_{bn}\frac{D_e - K^f}{K_a^d}$

(*) $\rho > 1$

Table 4.4 Parameters for numerical simulations

		Input and output market imperfectly competitive		
		Technology *a*	Technology *g*	Technology *AF*
r_i (tCO_2/MWh)	Scenario 1	0.8	0.4	0.5/0.8
	Scenario 2	0.5	0.4	<0.3
r_{bn} (tCO_2/MWh)			0.35	
ρ			1.1	
Inverse demand function			$p_e/c_a = 4 - 0.5 \cdot D_e(p)/D_e(c_a)$	

In addition, a numerical simulation is carried out for Scenario 1 (highly polluting supply) and Scenario 2 (cleaner supply).

The parameters related to these scenarios are described in Table 4.4.

From Tables 4.3 and 4.4, the results reported in Figs. 4.2 and 4.3 emerge for Scenario 1 and Scenario 2, respectively.

Finally, Table 4.5 summarizes the probability of decreasing market power in qualitative terms.

Then the following considerations arise:

1. Imperfect competition also in input markets decreases (increases) the probability of decreasing market power in Scenario 2 (Scenario 1);
2. When the dominant firm pursues a short-term profit target, decreasing market power is excluded with taxes and ETS with auctioning. It is admissible but relatively unlikely under ETS with benchmarking;
3. When the dominant firm pursues a long-term profit target (possible only under ETS), decreasing market power becomes more likely and very likely especially if allowances are benchmarked;
4. Decreasing market power is more likely if firms maximize profits rather than under regulatory pressure unless environmental regulation is based on ETS with benchmarking of emissions allowances.

5 Change in Prices and Pollution in Electricity Market

Looking at the short run, in fully competitive markets the environmental policy can modify the amount of pollutant emissions by means of two effects. On the one hand, it determines a decline in pollution as long as it causes an increase in prices and consequently a decrease in demand (and production). The increase in prices, and consequently the drop in demand, is related to the marginal cost of the marginal technology, that is to the emission rate of gas-fired plants and more polluting plants. On the other hand, if the pollution price is above the "switching price," it determines a switch of power producers on the merit order. This switch reduces significantly the production by the most polluting plants.

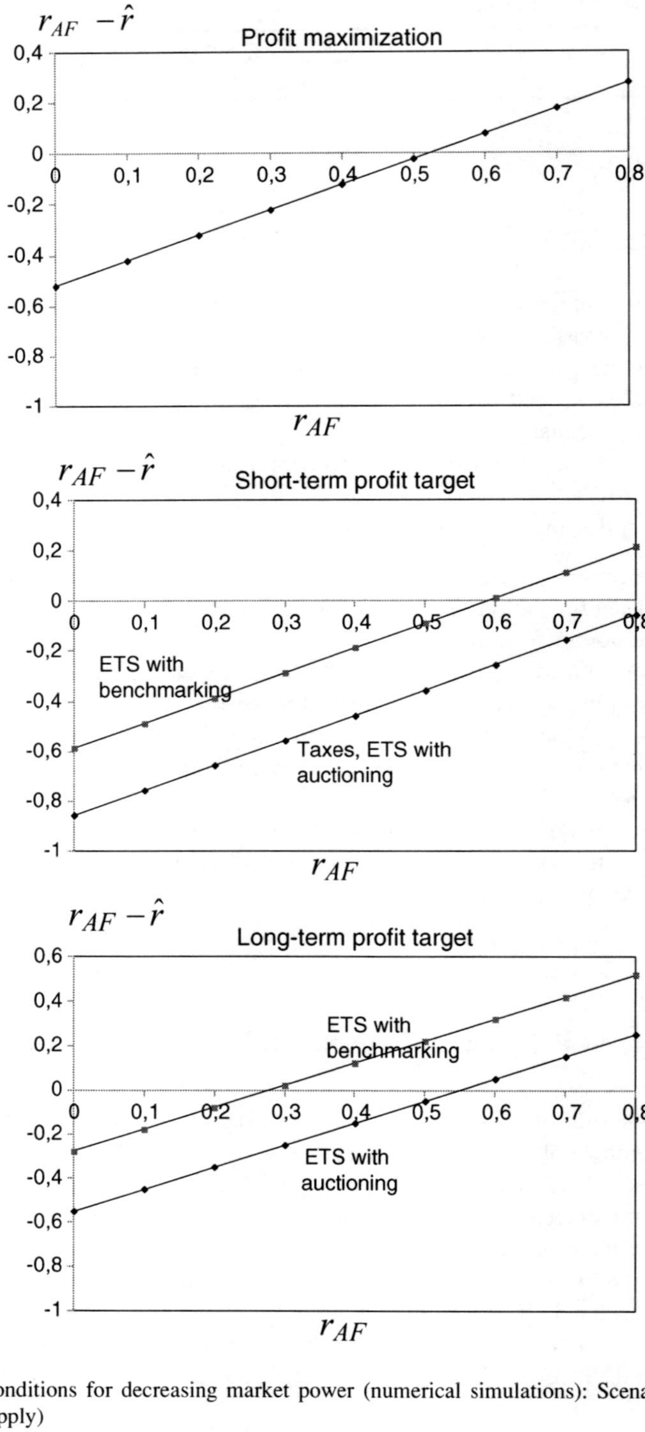

Fig. 4.2 Conditions for decreasing market power (numerical simulations): Scenario 1 (highly polluting supply)

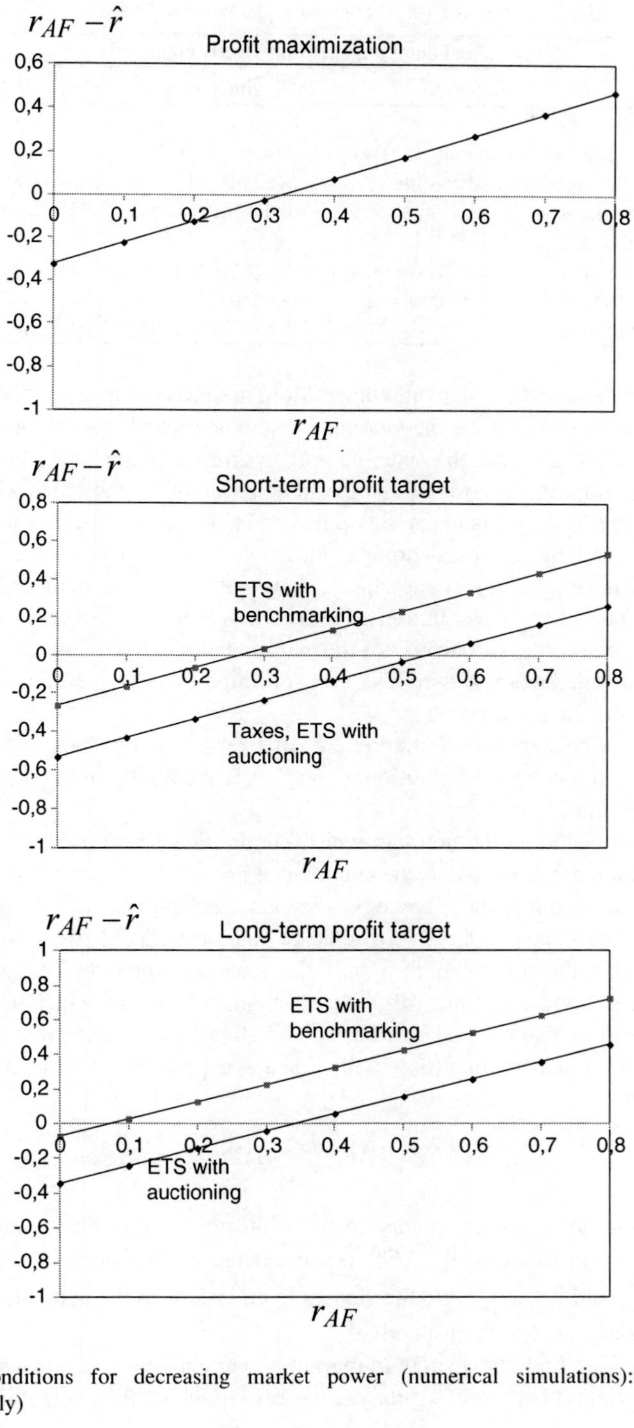

Fig. 4.3 Conditions for decreasing market power (numerical simulations): Scenario 2 (cleaner supply)

Table 4.5 Probability of decreasing market power (qualitative analysis)

	Input and output market imperfectly competitive		
	Pollution taxes	ETS with auctioning	ETS with benchmarking
Scenario 1			
Profit maximization	Admissible (likely)	Admissible (likely)	Admissible (likely)
Short-term profit target	Not admissible	Not admissible	Admissible (unlikely)
Long-term profit target		Admissible (likely)	Admissible (very likely)
Scenario 2			
Profit maximization	Admissible (unlikely)	Admissible (unlikely)	Admissible (unlikely)
Short-term profit target	Not admissible	Not admissible	Admissible (unlikely)
Long-term profit target		Admissible (unlikely)	Admissible (very likely)

It is to be noted that, under full competition, the increase in price depends on the change in marginal cost of the marginal technology and on the price elasticity of demand. In this analysis, the outcome is even simpler. Since "one-stepped" supply curve (constant marginal costs within the same group of technologies which implies very large steps of the cost curve) is assumed and since the price elasticity of demand is very low, carbon cost pass-through does not depend on the price elasticity of demand and is equal to the change in the marginal cost of the marginal technology provided that the change in pollution price is relatively low. In this case, therefore, the pass-through equals the carbon cost of the marginal unit in every hour. The same way of reasoning can be applied to the case of imperfect competition when prices converge to the marginal costs.

In imperfectly competitive markets, apart from these two possible effects, we should take into account an additional one that is the above-mentioned impact on the degree of market power.

This effect occurs in the hours in which the dominant firm modifies its strategy. These hours are denominated as the "on-change hours" while the remaining ones, in which the dominant firm's strategy remains unchanged, are denominated as "off-change hours" (Fig. 4.4). The off-change hours include: (1) the peak off-change hours in which the dominant firm bids the price threshold before and after the environmental policy; (2) the off-peak off-change hours in which the dominant firm bids the fringe's marginal cost before and after the environmental policy.

Overall imperfect competition will lessen the performance of environmental policy when

$$\Delta E_{ic} = \Delta E^{on} + \Delta E^{off}_{peak} + \Delta E^{off}_{off-peak} < \Delta E_{fc}$$

where ΔE_{ic} and ΔE_{fc} are the change in emissions under imperfect competition and full competition, respectively. ΔE^{on} is the change in emissions in the on-change hours. ΔE^{off}_{peak} and $\Delta E^{off}_{off-peak}$ are the change in emissions in the peak off-change and off-peak off-change hours, respectively.

To understand how the change in market power can impact on electricity prices and on pollution, it is helpful to analyze the case in which the leader holds only the

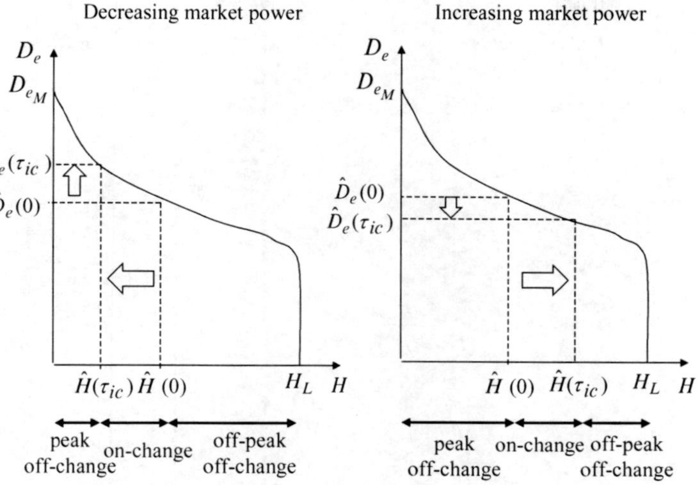

Fig. 4.4 Changes in market power

more polluting units (group a) and the fringe only the less polluting ones (group g), that is $\mu_a^{d_e} = 1$ and $\mu_a^{f_e} = 0$. These cases allow us to greatly simplify the graphical explanation without loss of generality.

Furthermore, for the sake of simplicity, we restrict the formal analysis (see below) only to the case in which $\tau < \tau^s$.

From Lemma 2 and Lemma 2bis, when $\mu_a^{d_e} = 1$ and $\mu_a^{f_e} = 0$, at the margin the load duration and change in price curves of Fig. 4.5 arise. It is to be noted that, when demand is less than the fringe's capacity (i.e., when the dominant firm and the fringe offer the same price, MC_{e_g}), only the dominant firm's plants (the most polluting and most efficient plants) are dispatched. This implicitly assumes the efficient rationing. However, with the proportional rationing and multiunit auctions the result would remain substantially unchanged.[7] At the same time, when demand is above the fringe's total capacity the rationing rule is not relevant since the dominant firm always bids below or above the marginal cost of the fringe.

The difference in marginal emissions between imperfect and full competition is given by (see Appendix):

[7] With multiunit auctions, strictly speaking, only offer prices of sets that may become marginal need to equal the system marginal price. Thus, proportional rationing has a negligible impact on pollution if the unit size is relatively small.

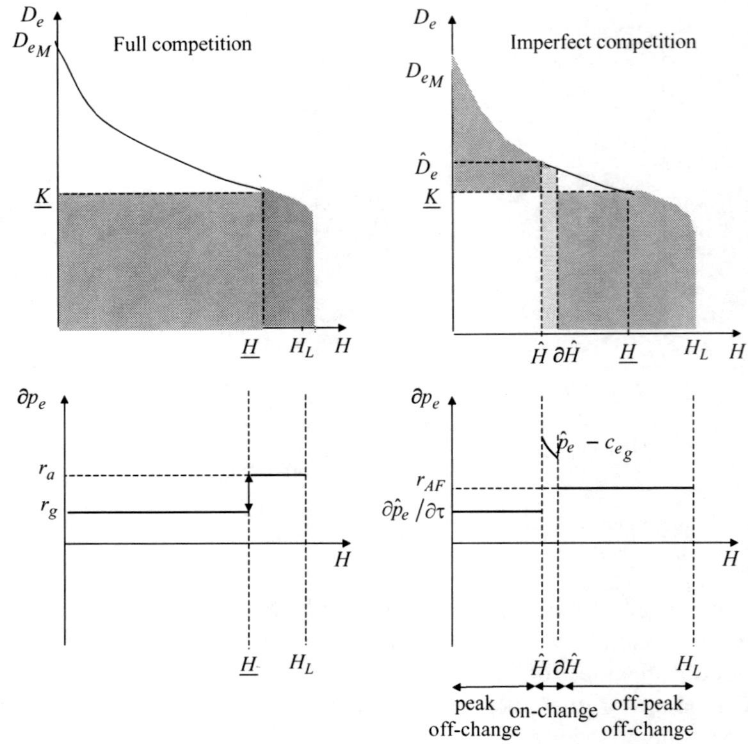

Fig. 4.5 Load duration and marginal price curves ($\mu_a^{d_e}=1$ and $\mu_a^{f_e}=0$): production by units of group a (*gray area*); production by units of group g (*white area*)

$$\frac{\partial E_{ic}}{\partial\tau}-\frac{\partial E_{fc}}{\partial\tau}=\underbrace{\left\{\underbrace{r_a\left[-\beta\frac{\partial\hat{p}_e}{\partial\tau}\int_0^{\hat{H}}D_e dH\right]}_{\text{Imperfect}}\underbrace{-r_g\left[-\beta r_g\int_0^{\hat{H}}D_e dH\right]}_{\text{Full}}\right\}}_{\text{peak off-change}}+$$

$$+\underbrace{\left\{\underbrace{(r_g-r_a)K_{e_T}\frac{\partial\hat{H}}{\partial\tau}-\hat{D}_e\left[\frac{\partial H}{\partial D_e}\left(\mp\beta(\hat{p}_e-MC_{AF})+\frac{\partial\hat{D}_e}{\partial\tau}\right)\right]}_{\text{Imperfect}}\underbrace{-\left[r_g(-\beta r_g)\left|\frac{\partial\hat{H}}{\partial\tau}\right|\right]}_{\text{Full}}\right\}}_{\text{on-change}}+$$

$$+\underbrace{\left\{\underbrace{r_g\left[-\beta r_{AF}\int_{\hat{H}}^{\underline{H}}D_e dH\right]+r_a\left[-\beta r_{AF}\int_{\underline{H}}^{H_L}D_e dH\right]}_{\text{Imperfect}}\underbrace{-r_g\left[-\beta r_g\int_{\hat{H}}^{\underline{H}}D_e dH\right]-r_a\left[-\beta r_a\int_{\underline{H}}^{H_L}D_e dH\right]}_{\text{Full}}\right\}}_{\text{off-peak off-change}}\tag{4.5}$$

The sign (+) (the sign (−)) in the on-change components of (4.5) refers to decreasing (increasing) market power.

By integrating over τ we get the total difference in the change in pollution:

$$\Delta E_{ic} - \Delta E_{fc} = \int_0^{\tau_{ic}} \frac{\partial E_{ic}}{\partial \tau} d\tau - \int_0^{\tau_{fc}} \frac{\partial E_{fc}}{\partial \tau} d\tau \tag{4.6}$$

where τ_{ic} and τ_{fc} are the pollution prices under imperfect competition and full competition, respectively. Obviously, under taxation the pollution price is exogenous, therefore $\tau_{ic} = \tau_{fc}$.

5.1 Without Regulatory Pressure

In Scenario 1, when $\mu_a^{d_e} = 1$ and $\mu_a^{f_e} = 0$ then $\partial \hat{H}/\partial \tau < 0$ if r_{AF} is sufficiently high. Consequently, the on-change component in (4.5) is positive. The marginal decrease in emissions under imperfect competition is lower (in absolute terms) than under full competition. By intuition, in the on-change hours the dominant firm will bid the price threshold and the marginal cost of the gas plant before and after the environmental regulation, respectively. Therefore, prices will sharply decrease. At the same time the change in the dominant firm's strategy has an impact on how the different technologies are dispatched (with their total capacity or not). After the implementation of the environmental policy, the dominant firm's units (the more polluting ones) will be dispatched with their total capacity, while the fringe will supply the residual demand. Together with the decrease in price, this will additionally involve a high increase in pollution.

It is to be noted that, if r_{AF} is sufficiently low, then $\partial \hat{H}/\partial \tau > 0$. In this case increasing pollution in on-change hours is excluded. Therefore, imperfect competition in input markets can significantly affect the probability of increasing pollution depending on the emissions rate of the alternative technology. However, since Scenario 1 is highly polluting we concentrate on the case of high r_{AF} that is on the case of decreasing market power $\partial \hat{H}/\partial \tau < 0$.

In the off-peak off-change hours, the corresponding component in (4.5) is surely positive ($r_{AF} < r_a$) if the share of more polluting plants is sufficiently high. Therefore, the marginal decrease in emissions is (in absolute terms) lower under imperfect competition than under full competition. In the peak off-change hours and with full competition, prices increase by r_g. Instead under imperfect competition and with linear demand, the price sensitivity to the pollution price is $\partial p_e^r/\partial \tau = 1/2 \cdot r_a$. Therefore, under the likely condition that $r_a \geq 2r_g$ (Scenario 1) the rise in prices under imperfect competition (and consequently the marginal decrease in emissions) is similar to that under full competition. Overall in the off-change hours, it is relatively likely that emissions decrease marginally less when markets are imperfectly competitive.

The difference in the total change in emissions (4.6) remains to be evaluated still. In case of ETS, this also requires to focus on the change in the pollution price. In this respect, we have to account for how the demand for allowances varies over time. In principle, lower marginal decrease in emissions leads to higher demand and consequently to higher pollution prices which can partially offset the change in emissions. Therefore, there will be a trade-off between marginal emissions and the change in pollution price. However, it is unlikely that this trade-off could nullify the difference in emissions between imperfect and full competition, for the following reason. The impact on pollution price of the change in demand by the power sector is relatively slight because total demand also depends on emissions in the other sectors covered by ETS. This is even more evident if a specific power sector within a multicountry ETS (as in the case of the EU-ETS) is considered.

Therefore, the pollution price is almost exogenous and the effect of marginal emissions is more important than the effect of the change in pollution price. Consequently, if the dominant firm holds a sufficiently high share of the more polluting units, emissions under imperfect competition will decrease less than under full competition, even in absolute terms. Obviously this is even more true under taxation where the pollution price is exogenous by definition. The overall results are described in Fig. 4.6 which compares the cases of full competition and imperfect competition. Three series of graphs are illustrated. The first and second series highlight the share of production by the two kinds of plants before (graphs A) and after (graphs B) the ETS implementation. The third series (graphs C) depicts the corresponding change in price curves.[8]

As noted, it is relatively likely that emissions decrease less under imperfect than under full competition. However, absolute increase in pollution is virtually excluded.

In Scenario 2, increasing market power is likely. In fact there is a high probability that the emissions rate of alternative fuel (low polluting) could be lower than the critical emissions rate (see Fig. 4.3). Consequently, in the on-change hours prices sharply increase and pollution sharply goes down. However, it is to be noted that the number of hours in which this can occur is relatively limited since the critical value of emissions rate, $\hat{r}$, is just above the expected emissions rate of alternative fuel, r_{AF} (see Fig. 4.3).

At the same time, in the off-peak off-change hours prices increase much less under imperfect competition (Fig. 4.7) while in the peak off-change hours the increase in prices may be significantly lower than that under full competition.

Consequently, emissions may decrease less under imperfect than full competition but the absolute increase in pollution is excluded.

[8] It is to be noted that, since we assume constant marginal costs for each category of plants (namely one-stepped supply curve), the increase in price under full competition is always equal to the full carbon cost of the marginal technology (full pass-through) except in the case where the demand curve intercepts the step of the supply curve (before and/or after regulation). However, the number of hours in which the pass-through rate is lower than one is almost negligible if the difference in marginal costs between technologies (the step) is relatively limited.

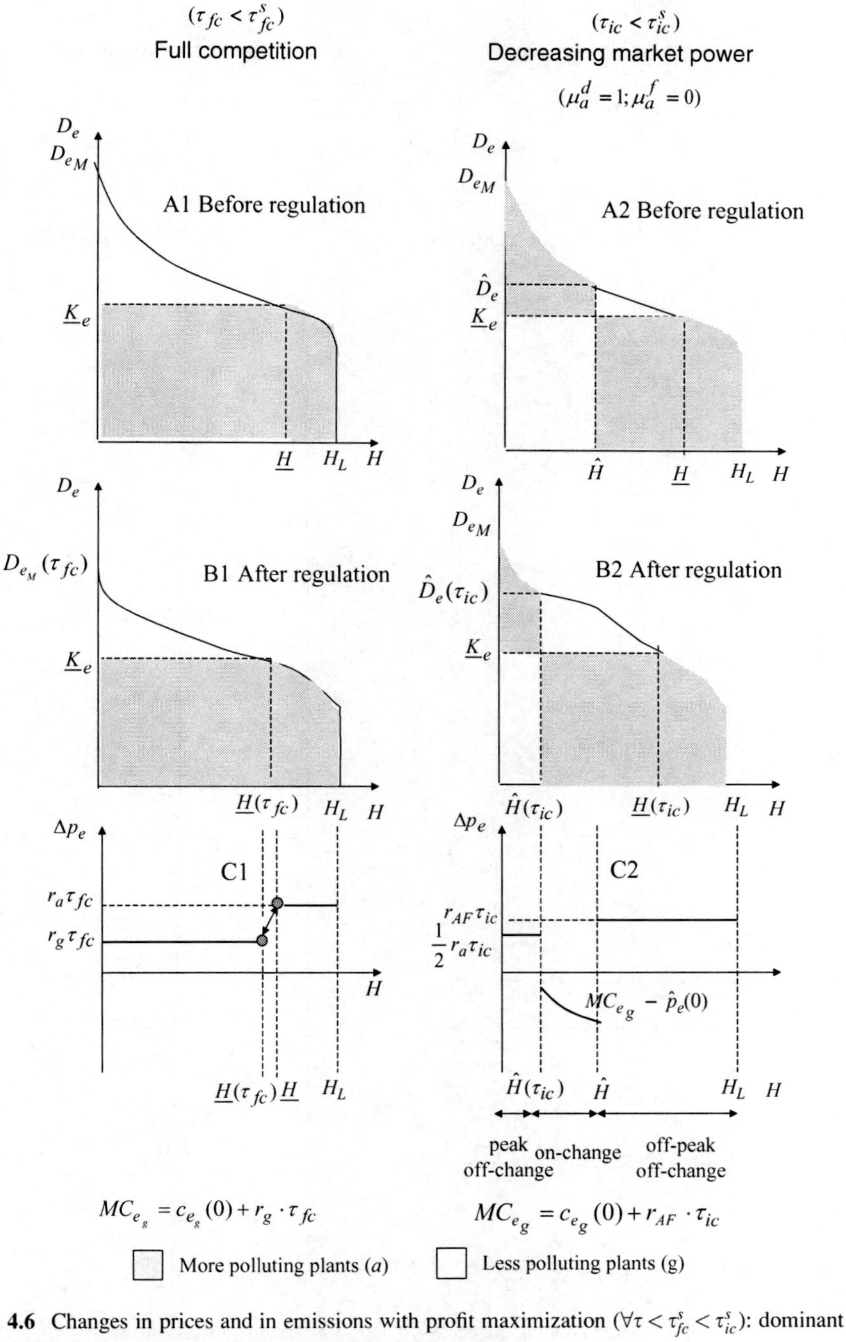

Fig. 4.6 Changes in prices and in emissions with profit maximization ($\forall \tau < \tau^s_{fc} < \tau^s_{ic}$): dominant firm owing only coal plants (Scenario 1 and short run)

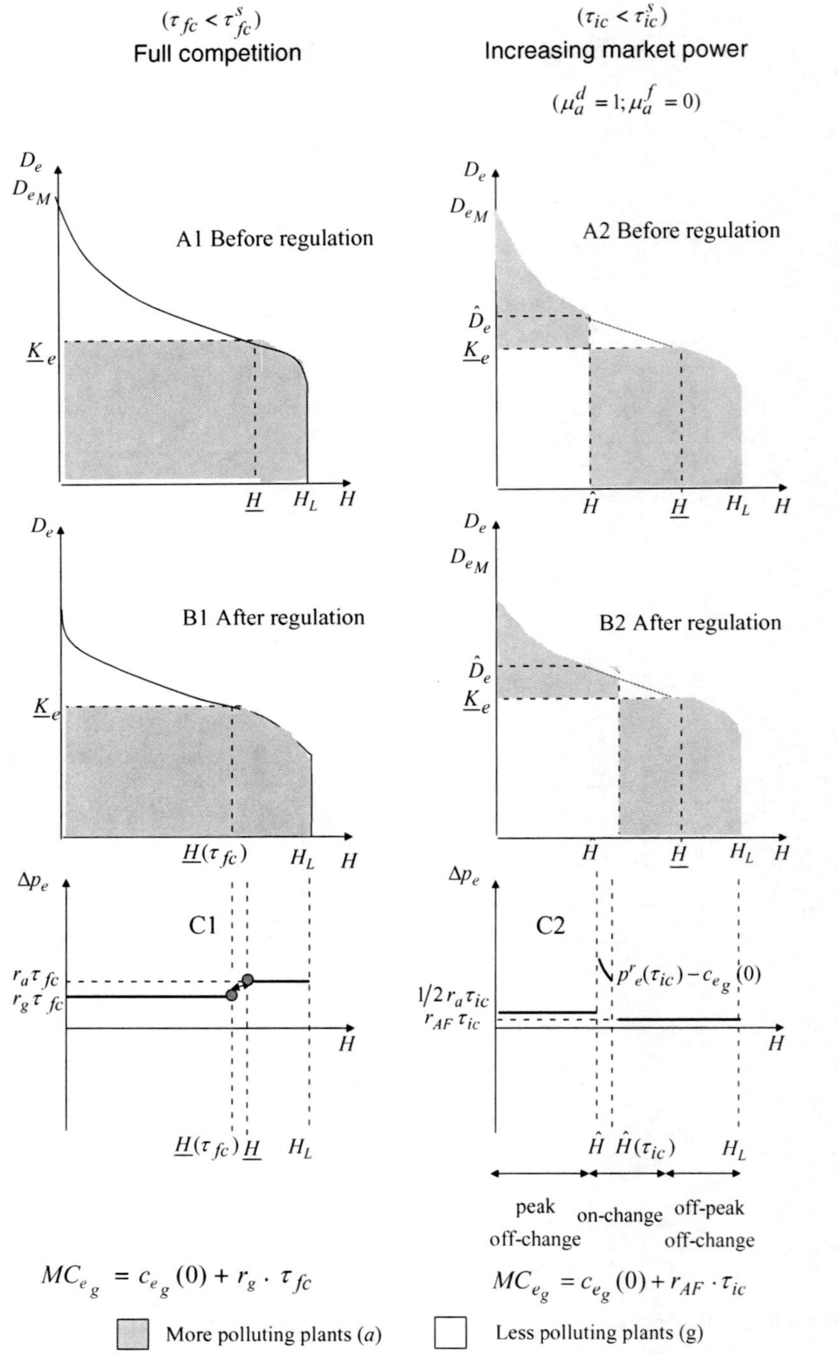

Fig. 4.7 Changes in prices and in emissions with profit maximization ($\forall \tau < \tau^s_{ic} < \tau^s_{fc}$): dominant firm owing only coal plants (Scenario 2 and short run)

However, we have also to consider that pollution prices can involve a switch of power producers on the merit order. Under imperfect competition in the input market, the "switching price" is $\tau_{ic}^{s} = (c_{e_g} - c_{e_a})/(r_a - r_{AF})$. Since under full competition $\tau_{fc}^{s} = (c_{e_g} - c_{e_a})/(r_a - r_g)$ then $\tau_{ic}^{s} < \tau_{fc}^{s}$, if the alternative fuel is a very low carbon fuel $(r_{AF} < r_g)$. This means that the induced change in merit order becomes more likely under imperfect than under full competition. In this case, the decrease in emissions under imperfect competition is higher than under full competition (Fig. 4.8).

In conclusion, on the one hand increasing pollution is virtually excluded in all cases. On the other hand, it is relatively likely that pollution can decrease less under imperfect competition than under full competition. However, in Scenario 2 this requires relatively low pollution prices.

These results are summarized in the following Proposition.

Proposition 2. *When the dominant firm can maximize profits, imperfect competition in both markets may lessen the performance of environmental policy especially if pollution prices are low. An absolute increase in pollution is virtually excluded.*

Proof. See discussion and graphical explanations above.

5.2 With Regulatory Pressure

In Scenario 1, under regulatory pressure and when $\mu_a^{d_e} = 1$ and $\mu_a^{f_e} = 0$, from Lemma 3bis (see the related proof in Appendix) and Corollary 4, then $\partial \hat{H}/\partial \tau < 0$ in two cases (Fig. 4.2): (1) with ETS if allowances are auctioned provided that firms pursue a long-term target or (2) under ETS especially if long-term targets combine with benchmarking of emissions allowances. We focus on this latter case where the on-change component in (4.5) is largely positive.

In the on-change hours after environmental policy implementation the dominant firm's units (the more polluting plants) will be dispatched with their total capacity. Together with the decrease in price, this will involve a sharp increase in pollution (see also graphs B2 and C2 of Fig. 4.9).

At the same time, the increase in price in the off-peak off change hours is under imperfect competition slightly lower than under full competition.

Instead, if allowances are benchmarked and firms pursue a long-term profit target the increase in price threshold under imperfect competition is very low (much lower than under full competition).

Consequently, the peak off-change component in (4.5) is largely negative and the off-peak off-change component is slightly negative.

Therefore, it is very likely that emissions decrease less under imperfect than full competition.

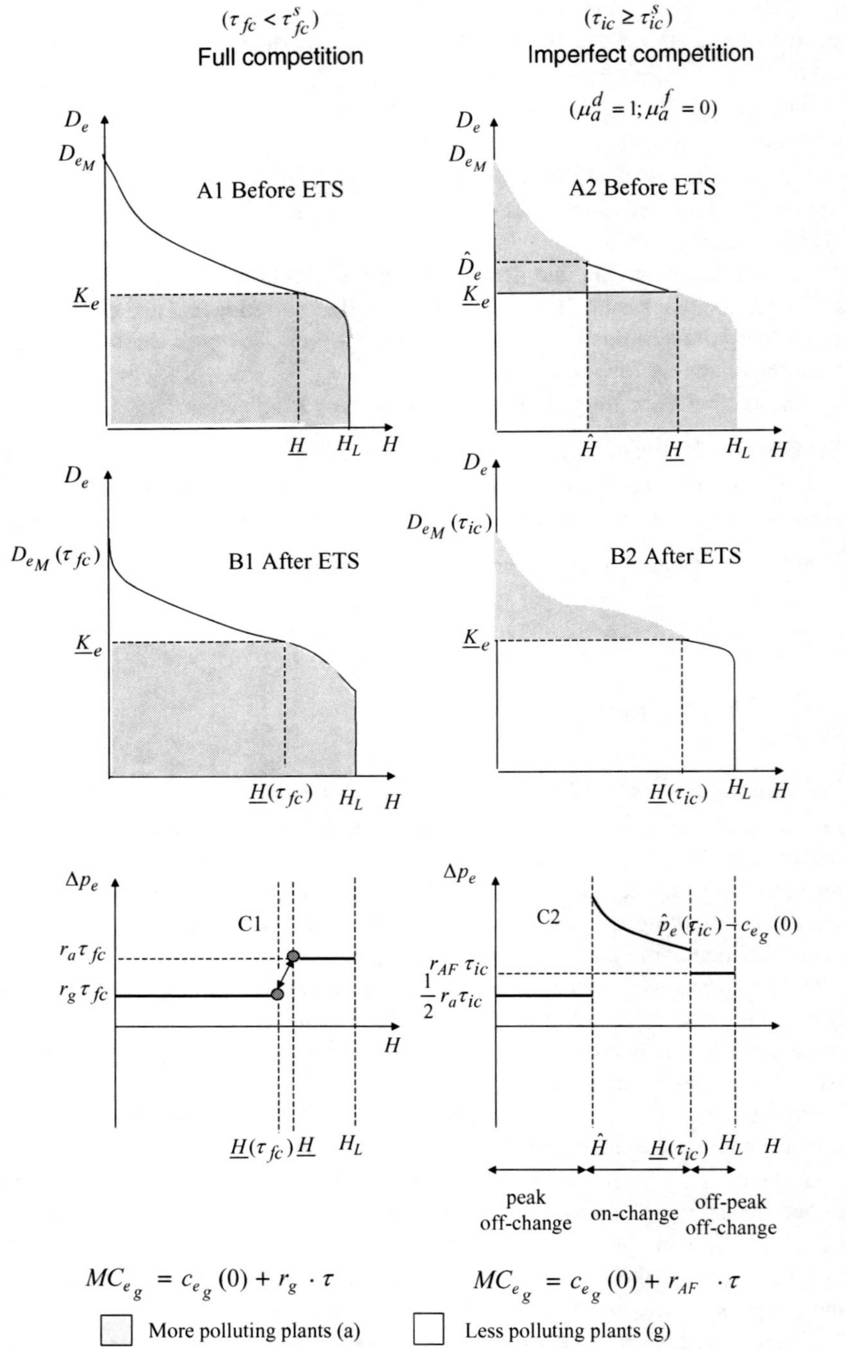

Fig. 4.8 Changes in prices and in emissions with profit maximization ($\tau^s_{ic} < \tau < \tau^s_{fc}$): Scenario 2 (short run)

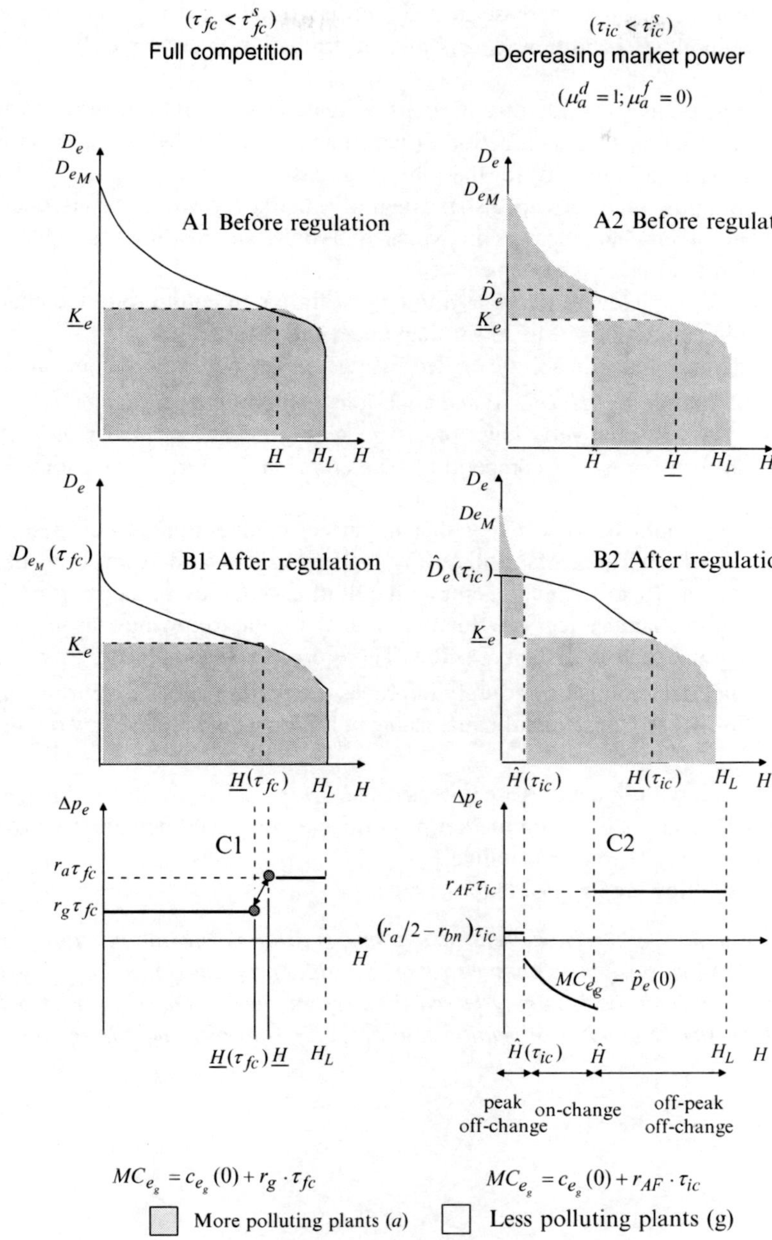

Fig. 4.9 Changes in prices and in emissions $\forall \tau < \tau_{fc}^{s} < \tau_{ic}^{s}$: long-term profit target with benchmarking (Scenario 1 and short run)

Nevertheless, absolute increase in pollution is virtually excluded unless under specific and unlikely conditions (the dominant firm holds a very large share of gas plants).

Furthermore, since marginally emissions decrease less, the pollution price would be higher under imperfect competition (more demand for allowances). However, this time there is no trade-off, for the following reason.

If the pollution price goes up, also the degree of market power, and consequently the number of on-change hours in which emissions sharply increase, goes up (see proof of Lemma 3bis in Appendix).

If this effect is relevant (large asymmetry of firms), in equilibrium the change (decrease) in emissions will be lower than under full competition.

In Scenario 2 the probability of decreasing market power is higher, at least apparently. Therefore, $\partial \hat{H} / \partial \tau < 0$ and emissions go up in the on-change hours.

Since r_{AF} is relatively low, prices increase much less under imperfect competition than under full competition. Therefore, in the former case emissions go up much less.

Overall it would be very likely that imperfect competition could lessen the performance of environmental policy (Fig. 4.10) and it would seem to be likely that it could lead to an absolute increase in pollution (but only in the short run[9]).

However, this latter effect is unlikely in reality for the following reason.

If r_{AF} is low (Scenario 2) then τ_{ic}^{s} is low. Therefore, it is likely that $\tau_{ic}^{s} < \tau < \tau_{fc}^{s}$. In this case imperfect competition surely improves the performance of environmental policies (Fig. 4.11). Consequently, increasing pollution would require low pollution prices.

However, if pollution prices are low then also $\partial \hat{H} / \partial \tau < 0$ is low in absolute terms (the number of hours in which market power decreases would be very restricted). Overall increasing pollution is unlikely.

Then the following Proposition arises.

Proposition 2bis. *In vertical related markets and for particular pollution price intervals (low prices), if firms pursue strategies besides profit maximization, imperfect competition in both markets may lessen the performance of environmental policy especially with ETS and free allocation of allowances. However, increasing pollution is unlikely.*

[9] On this issue, the economic literature provides a controversial framework. On the one hand, some authors find that the environmental policy never increases pollution. Among them, see Sugeta and Matsumoto (2007) and Canton et al. (2008). On the other hand, other authors (Levin 1985; Requate 2005) find that under imperfect competition the environmental policy can even increase emissions but only if specific conditions in terms of demand (extreme curvature) and supply (sufficiently asymmetric firms) are satisfied.

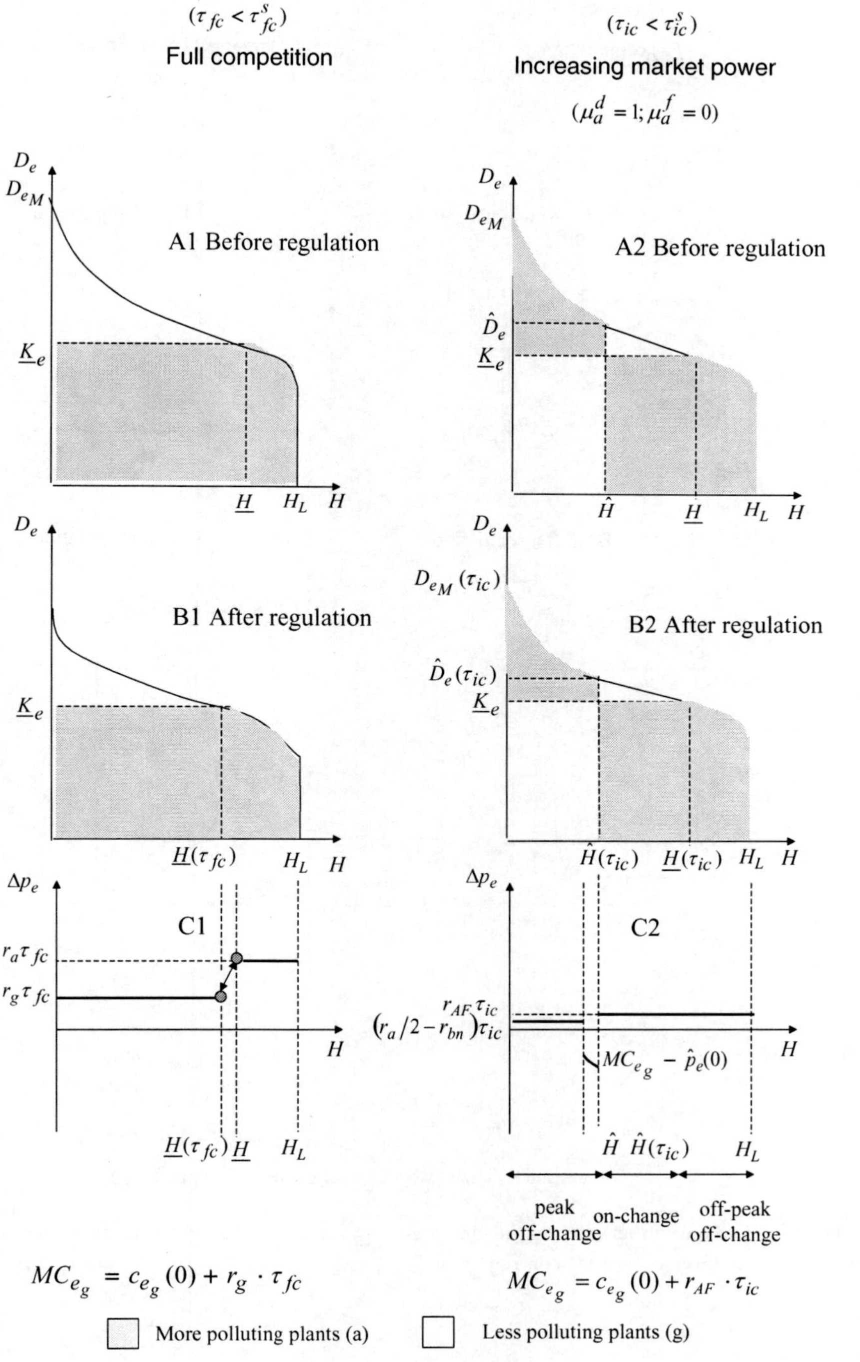

Fig. 4.10 Changes in prices and in emissions $\forall \tau < \tau^s_{ic} < \tau^s_{fc}$: long-term profit target with benchmarking (Scenario 2 and short run)

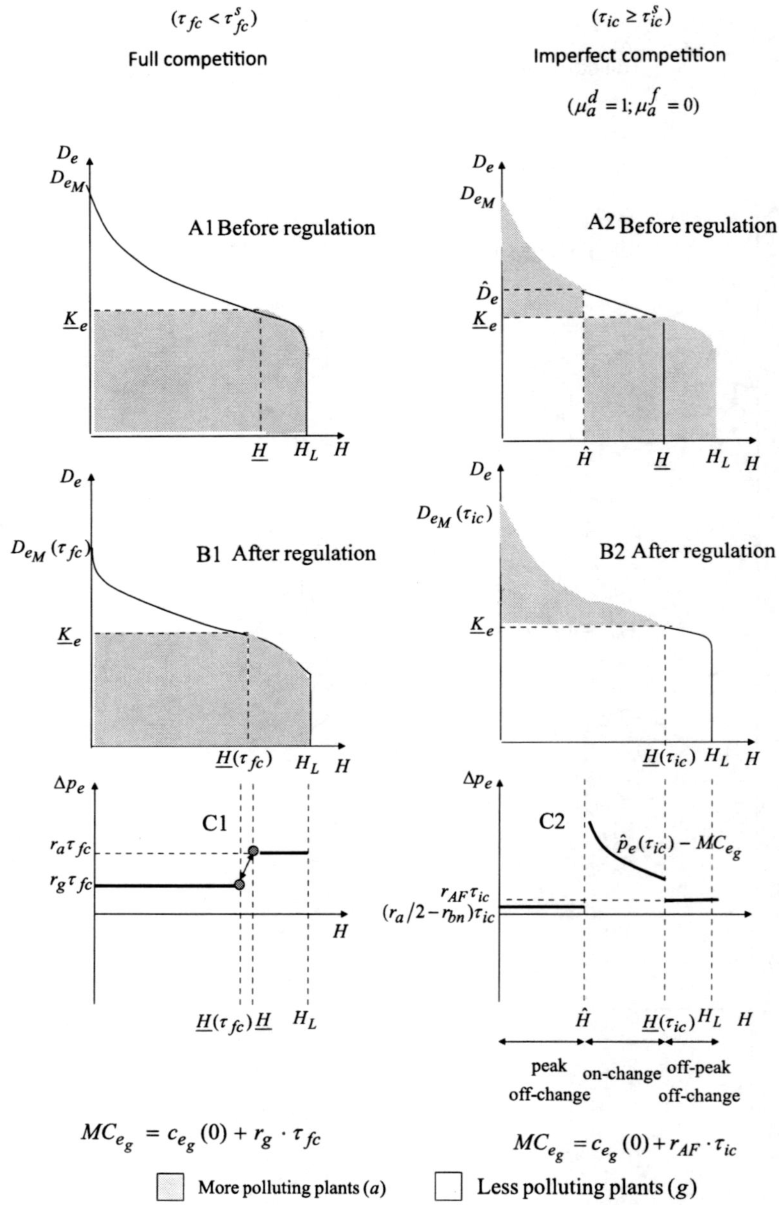

Fig. 4.11 Changes in prices and in emissions, $\tau^s_{fc} < \tau < \tau^s_{ic}$: long-term profit target with benchmarking (Scenario 2 and short run)

5.3 *Overall Framework*

Table 4.6 summarizes the results described in the previous subsections.

The following considerations arise:

1. When the dominant firm maximizes profits, it is likely that emissions could decrease less under imperfect competition that under full competition in Scenario 1. In Scenario 2 this can occur only if pollution prices are low. Absolute increase in pollution is virtually excluded in Scenario 2 or very unlikely in Scenario 1.
2. When the dominant firm pursues a short-term profit target, increasing pollution is admissible in Scenario 2 with ETS and benchmarking but only in principle. In fact this effect is unlikely. Since low pollution prices are necessary the number of hours in which market power decreases is low.
3. When the dominant firm pursues a long-term profit target (admissible only under ETS), emissions may increase less under imperfect competition especially in Scenario 2 with benchmarking but provided that pollution prices are very low. Furthermore, although in this specific case absolute increase in pollution might seem to be likely, its probability to occur is relatively low. In fact, once again, since low pollution prices are necessary, the number of hours in which market power decreases is restricted.

6 About the Assumptions and the Robustness of the Results

The results described earlier depend on a series of simple assumptions about the structure and operation of energy markets, namely hypotheses about technologies, competition models, firms' strategies and market structures. Before concluding, it is important to discuss them in order to check the robustness of the analysis.

6.1 *Isoelastic Demand*

In this analysis we make two fundamental assumptions about the power demand function. There is no uncertainty (deterministic demand). The (inverse) demand curve is linear.

The first assumption is consistent with the fact that we consider firms to make bids valid for short periods of time (they bids for each hour) when demand does not vary significantly during the period of time for which the bid is valid.

The second assumption has an important implication. With linear demand the residual monopoly price raises less than the marginal cost (pass-through less than one), whereas with isoelastic demand the changes in (the residual monopoly) prices would be larger than the changes in marginal costs.

Table 4.6 Impact on pollution

	Decrease in emissions lower under imperfect competition					
	Pollution taxes		ETS with auctioning		ETS with benchmarking	
	Scenario 1	Scenario 2	Scenario 1	Scenario 2	Scenario 1	Scenario 2
Profit maximization	Admissible (likely)	Admissible (very low pollution prices)	Admissible (likely)	Admissible (very low pollution prices)	Admissible (likely)	Admissible (very low pollution prices)
Short-term profit target	Admissible (very unlikely)	Admissible (unlikely)	Admissible (very unlikely)	Admissible (unlikely)	Admissible (unlikely)	Admissible (very low pollution prices)
Long-term profit target			Admissible (unlikely)	Admissible (very low pollution prices)	Admissible (unlikely)	Admissible (very low pollution prices)
	Increasing pollution					
	Pollution taxes		ETS with auctioning		ETS with benchmarking	
Profit maximization	Admissible (very unlikely)	Not admissible	Admissible (very unlikely)	Not admissible	Admissible (very unlikely)	Not admissible
Short-term profit target	Not admissible	Not admissible	Not admissible	Not admissible	Admissible (very unlikely)	Admissible (very unlikely)
Long-term profit target			Admissible (unlikely)	Admissible (very unlikely)	Admissible (very unlikely)	Admissible (unlikely)

Thus, on the one hand, this reinforces the result that increasing pollution is unlikely. However, on the other hand, isoelastic demand might make it less likely that imperfect competition could lessen the performance of environmental policy (compared to full competition).

6.2 *Variable Marginal Costs*

As pointed out before, a fundamental assumption of the model is that power plants are homogeneous within the same group of technologies. This assumption does not reflect the real conditions of operation for two reasons. First, power generation costs include cycling costs which vary with the level of demand. Second, power stations may have different fuel costs even if they belong to the same group of technologies (using the same fuel).

The cycling cost is the additional cost of power generation when the generation unit is operating on margin, that is when the generation unit meets varying demand and consequently has to adjust its output frequently, including frequent start-ups and shut-downs. The cost of cycling depends on the type of technology. Cycling involves increasing costs due to higher fuel costs and component degradation. The level of this additional cost depends on the type of technology. For example, it is higher for coal plants than for gas plants. By using the analysis carried out by Denny and O'Malley (2009), it is possible to estimate the cycling costs of a system including coal and gas units in the same proportion (50 % coal and 50 % gas). Within this system, the cycling cost is about 6 and 10 Euro/MWh when the gas plants and the coal plants operate on the margin, respectively. This component is important because it makes the strategic behavior more expensive. In fact, the dominant firm could not follow a strategy in which it actually reduced output once the level of demand became high enough to support a supposed equilibrium at the maximum price. The level of output from power stations is expensive to adjust, particularly if the required pattern would involve reducing output at first and then increasing it as demand rises further.

Therefore, neglecting cycling cost and assuming homogeneous plants (within the same group of technologies) imply that the marginal cost curve in our model is "one-stepped," and not a quasi-continuous increasing curve. As pointed out before, this assumption is not realistic but it does not undermine the significance of the analysis for the following reasons.

Firstly, looking at the case of imperfect competition, accounting for cycling costs and plants' nonhomogeneity modifies $\underline{MC}$ and $\overline{MC}$ and consequently the value of ζ and σ so changing just the value of $\hat{D}_e$ (and consequently the impact on the degree of market power) but not its structure[10] (see Lemma 2 and Lemma 2bis).

[10] For instance, looking at the simplified case in which $\mu_a^{d_e} = 1$ and $\mu_a^{f_e} = 0$, $\overline{MC}_e$ will be the marginal cost (including cycling cost) of the marginal unit (the unit setting price), i.e. the last fringe's unit dispatched. $\underline{MC}_e$ will be the average marginal cost of the dominant firm's most efficient units.

Secondly, looking at the case of full competition, the pass-through will be just lower than the marginal cost of the marginal technology provided that the price elasticity of demand in the short run is relatively low, as assumed in this analysis and consistently with the real situation of electricity markets.

Finally, variable (increasing) fringe's marginal costs may imply that the dominant firm accommodates only a portion of fringe's supply even when it bids the residual monopoly price. This latter depends on the shape of the fringe's cost curve which in turn depends on the pollution price. This means that prices not necessarily jump from the price threshold to the fringe's marginal cost but that the price profile is continuous (or quasi-continuous) from the former to the latter. Consequently, the effect on pollution will be gradual (and less evident) but its sign remains unchanged.

6.3 Other Market Structures

The dominant firm model is generally used in the literature on the environmental policy under imperfect competition [see Conrad and Wang (1993), Chernyavs'ka and Gulli (2008a, b) and Gulli (2008)]. On the methodological side, the attraction of this characterization is that it avoids the implausible extreme of perfect competition and pure monopoly, at the same time escaping the difficulties of characterizing an oligopolistic equilibrium. In particular, this model allows us to overcome the problem of possible inexistent equilibria in pure strategy (see below). Moreover, in investigating strategic bidding in electricity pools, Garcia-Diaz and Marin (2003) find that very strong asymmetries lead to a single equilibrium price with a dominant firm where small firms behave competitively.

However, many natural gas and electricity markets have characteristics which can be better simulated by using oligopolistic models.

With regards to the gas market, in a duopolistic framework if both firms are capacity unconstrained the net long-run marginal cost of the alternative fuel is a pure-strategy equilibrium only with efficient rationing and if capacities are sufficiently small, i.e., the price that clears all capacity is higher than the net long-run marginal cost of the alternative fuel. Instead if the cost-leader is capacity unconstrained or both firms are capacity constrained and capacities are sufficiently high, i.e., such that the price that clears all capacity is lower than the net long-run marginal cost of the alternative fuel, the equilibrium is generally unique but in nondegenerate mixed strategies.

With regards to the electricity market, in their article on spot market competition in the UK electricity industry, using a typical duopolistic framework and the auction approach, von der Fehr and Harbord (1993) demonstrate the following:

1. If the demand is high, higher than the capacity of the largest generator, "prices always equal the highest admissible price." However, the low bidding generator may be either the high-cost or the low-cost generator so we cannot know which of them is dispatched with its total or part of its capacity. Instead under the dominant firm we know that, above (below) a certain level of demand, the high-cost generator is dispatched with its total (part of) capacity.

2. If the demand is low, lower than the capacity of the smallest generator, prices are always equal to the marginal cost of the less efficient generator. In this case only the low-cost generator will produce consistently with the outcome of the dominant firm model.
3. When demand is "intermediate," lower than the capacity of the largest generator but higher than that of the smallest one, there are equilibria only in mixed strategies in which prices are in between a lowest price and the maximum admissible price. The lowest price is strictly greater than the marginal cost of the least efficient generator. Furthermore, it is increasing in demand and converging to the maximum price when demand converges to the capacity of the largest generator (case 1 above) and to the marginal cost of the low-cost generator when demand converges to the capacity of the latter. Furthermore, the lowest price is an increasing function of the marginal cost of the less efficient generator. This outcome is consistent with the results of the dominant firm model. In fact, on the one hand, when demand is relatively high we expect that the carbon cost pass-through will be affected by the price threshold sensitivity to the carbon price. On the other hand, when demand is relatively low, we expect that the pass-through will be more affected by the carbon cost of the less efficient generator. The only difference is that in the dominant firm model the price profile is discrete, jumping from the marginal cost of the low-cost generator to the price threshold. In the duopoly model this profile is continuous since prices move gradually from the cost of the low-cost generator to the price threshold. Instead, once again, as suggested by von der Fehr and Harbord, we cannot know which generator will be the high-bidding generator. The high-cost generator will generally submit higher bids than the low-cost generator but there is a positive significant probability that the high-cost generator becomes the only operating generator.

Then, given this framework, it is possible to conclude that the results of the dominant firm model can be only partially generalized to other market structures (namely duopolistic). The price profile seems to be very similar. In the periods of high demand prices equal the price threshold, while in those of relatively low demand prices equal the marginal cost of the high-cost generator. In the intermediate periods prices are above and an increasing function of the marginal cost of the less efficient generator converging to the price threshold as long as demand increases. Therefore, the mechanisms through which the pollution price is passed through to electricity prices are very similar. Instead the dispatching is ambiguous (which generator is the low or high-bidding generator). The results of the dominant firm model can be partially generalized only when, within the duopolistic model, the probability that the low-cost generator will be the high-bidding generator increases in demand.[11]

[11] In the variable demand periods, von der Fehr and Harbord (1993, 1998) demonstrate that the "high-cost generator profile stochastically dominates the strategy profile of the low-cost generator. Thus, the high-cost generator will generally (i.e. in expected terms) submit higher bids than the

6.4 Other Types of Free Allocation

The basic model considers just two kinds of allowance allocation: auctioning and benchmarking. These are the most common methods used for allocation of permits. They are the only two considered for the EU ETS post 2012. Nevertheless, in the first and second phase of the EU ETS (before 2012), auctioning was limited: only 5 % in the first phase and 10 % in the second one. Furthermore, many countries used different forms of grandfathering preferring it to benchmarking. The allowances were allocated to different power technologies on the basis of their typical emissions rate and on the basis of their past (or expected) amount of electricity generation.

In this case, from (4.2bis), the change in the gas price becomes

$$\begin{aligned}\left(\frac{dp_g}{d\tau}\right)_{ETS} &= \eta_g \frac{dc_{e_g}}{d\tau} = \eta_g\left[(r_{AF} - r_g) + r_g\alpha_g - r_{AF}\alpha_{AF}\right] \\ &= \left(\frac{dp_g}{d\tau}\right)_{bn} + \eta_g\left(r_g\alpha_g - r_{AF}\alpha_{AF}\right)\end{aligned} \tag{4.7}$$

with

$\alpha_j = \bar{E}_j / E_j$ is the ratio of allocation for the fuel $j = AF, g$

Then the following cases arise:

1. Free allocation with benchmarking. This method was already considered in the basic model. In this case $\alpha_g = \alpha_{AF} r_{AF} / r_g$ and consequently $\frac{dc_{e_g}}{d\tau} = \left(\frac{dc_{e_g}}{d\tau}\right)_{bn}$.
2. Free allocation with updating. It implies that $\bar{E}_{AF}$ is just below E_{AF} and $\bar{E}_g$ is just below E_g. As a consequence $\alpha_g \cong \alpha_{AF} \cong 1$. Therefore, $\frac{dc_{e_g}}{d\tau} < \left(\frac{dc_{e_g}}{d\tau}\right)_{bn}$ if $r_g < r_{AF}$ and vice versa.
3. Free allocation with grandfathering and relative under-allocation. In this case $\alpha_g < \alpha_{AF} r_{AF} / r_g$. Consequently, $\frac{dc_{e_g}}{d\tau} < \left(\frac{dc_{e_g}}{d\tau}\right)_{bn}$.
4. Free allocation with grandfathering and relative over-allocation. In this case $\alpha_g > \alpha_{AF} r_{AF} / r_g$. Therefore, $\frac{dc_{e_g}}{d\tau} > \left(\frac{dc_{e_g}}{d\tau}\right)_{bn}$.

low-cost generator". However, looking at the strategy probability distributions of the two firms, the extent to which the strategy profile of the high-cost generator dominates that of the low-cost generator decreases in demand. Consequently, we expect that the probability that the high-cost generator will be the high-bidding generator decreases in demand.

5. Free allocation with grandfathering and absolute (homogeneous) over-allocation. It implies that $\alpha_g = \alpha_{AF} > 1$. Therefore, $\frac{dc_{e_g}}{d\tau} < \left(\frac{dc_{e_g}}{d\tau}\right)_{bn}$ if $r_g < r_{AF}$ and vice versa.

Finally compared to benchmarking the condition for decreasing market power (with regulatory pressure)

$$\partial\hat{p}_e/\partial\tau < \hat{r} = r_a + \lambda(r_g - r_a + dc_{e_g}/d\tau),$$

is more likely to be satisfied (1) with relative over-allocation and (2) with updating and absolute over-allocation if the alternative fuel is low polluting. This condition is less likely to be satisfied with updating and absolute over-allocation if the alternative fuel is high polluting.

7 Conclusions

This chapter identifies the mechanisms through which imperfect competition in vertical related energy markets (electricity and natural gas markets) can affect the performance of environmental policy (its ability to reduce pollution and/or its ability to reduce pollution minimizing the cost of meeting environmental targets). The change in emissions under imperfect competition can be quite different than under full competition for several reasons: (1) imperfect and full competition can be different in how environmental regulation impacts on the marginal costs of the power technologies; they can be different in how the change in cost is passed-through to prices; (3) under imperfect competition the change in cost structure between technologies determines a change in market power.

By using the dominant firm model (in both markets) and the auction approach (in electricity markets), the analysis shows that the pollution cost of the gas-fired plants does not depend on their own emission rate but on that of their main alternative.

Then imperfect competition may lessen the ability of environmental policy to reduce pollution (in the short run).

In principle this would occur regardless of the power supply scenario (Scenario 1 or Scenario 2) and regardless of the kind of environmental regulation (whether based on pollution taxes or on emissions trading and, in the latter case, regardless of the type of allowance allocation, whether based on auctioning or benchmarking).

However, in Scenario 2 it can occur only if pollution prices are relatively low and, in both scenarios, it seems to be more likely when firms can maximize profits rather than under regulatory pressure (unless firms pursue long-term profit targets and environmental regulation is based on ETS with benchmarking).

The analysis also highlights that an absolute increase in pollution, at least in the short run, cannot be excluded not only in specific time periods (specific groups of hours of electricity demand) but also considering the entire power demand cycle.

Nevertheless, it is important to point out that it is unlikely even when firms pursue a long-term profit target and regulation is based on ETS and benchmarking of emissions allowances. Therefore, increasing pollution is virtually excluded.

Summing up, this analysis suggests that, in order to estimate the real economic impact of environmental policy and its real effectiveness, analysts should take accurately into account the effect of imperfect competition in energy markets. In fact, as this work seems to suggest, imperfect competition can significantly affect the performance of environmental policy as long as it has impact on product prices, on how the different polluting plants are dispatched and, consequently, on aggregate emissions. Then if analysts neglect the role of imperfect competition, policymakers may set incorrect environmental targets, when these targets are chosen also taking into account the cost of environmental policy.

Finally it is worth underlying that the results of this chapter are based on a series of simple assumptions about the operation of energy markets. Nevertheless, they seem to be enough robust, although the analysis suggests caution in extending to other market structures the outcome of the dominant firm model.

Appendix

Proof of Lemma 2

Let $\bar{K}_e = D_{e_M} - \bar{K}_e^{d_e}$ be the peak demand minus the dominant firm's capacity in least efficient plants ($\bar{K}_e^{d_e}$) with $\bar{H} = D^{-1}(\bar{K}_e)$. It is immediately intuitive that when $D_e \geq \bar{K}_e$ the system marginal price equals the price threshold, $\hat{p}_e$. When $D_e \leq \underline{K}_e^{f_e}$, pure Bertrand equilibria (first marginal cost pricing) arise and prices equal the marginal cost of the most efficient plants ($\underline{MC}_e$).

In fact, on the one hand, whenever the demand is so high that both leader's and the fringe's least efficient units can enter the market, the dominant firm would not gain any advantage by competing à la Bertrand, i.e., by attempting to undercut the rivals. Therefore, it will maximize its profit by bidding the residual monopoly price.

On the other hand, whenever the power demand is lower than the fringe's power capacity in most efficient plants, competing à la Bertrand is the only leader's available strategy in order to have a positive probability of entering the market. As a consequence, prices will converge to the marginal cost of the most efficient plants.

It remains to identify the leader's optimal choice on $D_e \in \left]\bar{K}_e; \underline{K}_e^{f_e}\right]$.[12] Under the assumptions of the model, each firm in the competitive fringe has a unique

[12] It is to be noted that assuming a dominant firm with competitive fringe model, rather than an oligopolistic framework, ensures that equilibria in pure strategy do exist. For an explanation of why equilibria in pure strategies do not exist in the case of oligopolistic competition, see von der Fehr and Harbord (1993, 1998).

dominant strategy regardless of the market demand: bidding according to its own marginal cost of production. By converse the best choice of the dominant firm might consist in (i) bidding the price threshold ($\hat{p}_e$) or in (ii) bidding $\overline{MC}_e$.[13]

Let $\pi_A^{d_e}$ and $\pi_B^{d_e}$ be the profits corresponding to the first and second strategies above, respectively. Whenever the least efficient units could enter the market (i.e., $D_e \geq \underline{K}_e$), the profit the dominant firm earns by choosing the first strategy (i.e., $\forall H \in]\bar{H};\underline{H}]$) is

$$\pi_A^{d_e} = (\hat{p}_e - \underline{MC}_e)[D_e - (1-\delta)K_{e_T}] + \sum\nolimits_{i=1}^{z} \sum\nolimits_{j=a,b} \tau \cdot r_{bn} \cdot \bar{q}_j^i \tag{4.8}$$

Where

r_{bn} =emission rate of the technology chosen as the benchmark

$\bar{q}_j^i$ = reference production for the free allocation of allowances to the *i-th* unit belonging to the group *j* of plants. Obviously $\bar{q}_j^i = 0$ with full auctioning.

If the dominant firm chooses the second strategy, he earns

$$\pi_B^{d_e} = (\overline{MC}_e - \underline{MC}_e)\underline{K}_e^{d_e} + \sum\nolimits_{i=1}^{z} \sum\nolimits_{j=a,b} \tau \cdot r_{bn} \cdot \bar{q}_j^i \tag{4.9}$$

Let C_{e_d} the dominant firm's total cost. When the dominant firm maximizes profits, $\hat{p}_e$ is the residual monopoly price with

$$\hat{p}_e = p_e^r = \arg\max_{p_e}\{p_e[D_e(p_e) - K^{f_e}] - C_{e_d}\} = \frac{1}{\beta}[D_e - (1-\delta)K_{e_T}] + \underline{MC}_e$$

if the share of most efficient plant operated by the dominant firm is large enough. It is to be noted that by differentiating this equation with respect to τ and when $\tau < \tau^s$, then $\dfrac{\partial p_e^r}{\partial \tau} = \dfrac{r_a}{2}$.

Consequently $\pi_A^{d_e} \geq \pi_B^{d_e}$ if and only if

$$D_e \geq \hat{D}_{e_1} = \left[\underline{\mu}^{d_e}\delta\zeta + (1-\delta)\right]K_{e_T} \tag{4.10}$$

Where $\zeta = \dfrac{\overline{MC}_e - \underline{MC}_e}{p_e^r - \underline{MC}_e}$ and $\beta = -\dfrac{dD_e}{dp_e}$

When $D_e \in \left]\underline{K}_e; \underline{K}_e^{f_e}\right]$ (i.e., $H \in \left]\underline{H}, \underline{H}^{f_e}\right]$) the profit the dominant firm earns by choosing the first strategy is

[13] Strictly speaking, bidding $\overline{MC}_e$ for units of kind b and $\hat{p}_e \leq \overline{MC}_e - \varepsilon$ (where $\varepsilon \cong 0^+$) for units of kind a.

$$\pi_C^{d_e} = (p_e^r - \underline{MC}_e)[D_e - (1-\delta)K_{e_T}] + \sum_{i=1}^{z} \sum_{j=a,b} \tau \cdot r_{bn} \cdot \bar{q}_j^i \tag{4.11}$$

and by choosing the second strategy the profit is

$$\pi_D^{d_e} = (\overline{MC}_e - \underline{MC}_e)\left[D_e - \underline{\mu}^{f_e}(1-\delta)K_{e_T}\right] + \sum_{i=1}^{z} \sum_{j=a,b} \tau \cdot r_{bn} \cdot \bar{q}_j^i \tag{4.12}$$

Thus, the dominant firm will choose the first strategy if and only if $\pi_C^{d_e} \geq \pi_D^{d_e}$, i.e., if and only if

$$D_e \geq \hat{D}_{e_2} = (1-\delta)\left[\frac{1-\zeta\underline{\mu}^{f_e}}{1-\zeta}\right]K_{e_T} \tag{4.13}$$

Finally by differentiating $\hat{D}_e$ with respect to $\underline{\mu}^{d_e}$ and $\underline{\mu}^{f_e}$ we get

$$\frac{\partial \hat{D}_{e_1}}{\partial \underline{\mu}^d} = \delta\ \zeta\ K_{e_T} > 0$$

and

$$\frac{\partial \hat{D}_{e_2}}{\partial \underline{\mu}^f} = -K_{e_T}(1-\delta)\frac{\zeta}{1-\zeta} < 0$$

Proof of Lemma 3

The derivative of $\hat{D}_e$ with respect to τ can be written as

$$\frac{\partial \hat{D}_e}{\partial \tau} = \frac{\partial \hat{D}_e}{\partial \zeta}\frac{\partial \zeta}{\partial \tau} \tag{4.14}$$

Since [from (4.10) and (4.13)]

$$\frac{\partial \hat{D}_{e_1}}{\partial \sigma} = \underline{\mu}^{d_e} \cdot \delta \cdot K_{e_T} > 0 \tag{4.15a}$$

and

$$\frac{\partial \hat{D}_{e_2}}{\partial \zeta} = \frac{(1-\delta)(1-\underline{\mu}^{f_e})}{(1-\zeta)^2} K_{e_T} > 0 \tag{4.15b}$$

then the degree of market power is a decreasing function of ζ.

By differentiating ζ with respect to τ and given that $\hat{p}_e$ and c_{e_g} depend on τ, we get

$$\frac{\partial \zeta}{\partial \tau} = \frac{1}{(p_e^r - c_{e_a} - r_a\tau)^2}\left[(r_{AF} - r_a)(p_e^r(0) - c_{e_a}) - (\partial p_e^r/\partial \tau - r_a)(c_{e_g}(0) - c_{e_a})\right] \tag{4.16}$$

if $\tau < \tau^s$.

and

$$\frac{\partial \zeta}{\partial \tau} = \frac{1}{(p_e^r - c_{e_g} - r_g\tau)^2}\left[(r_a - r_{AF})(p_e^r(0) - c_{e_g}(0)) - (\partial p_e^r/\partial \tau - r_{AF})(c_{e_a} - c_{e_g}(0))\right] \tag{4.17}$$

if $\tau \geq \tau^s$.

From (4.16), since $\frac{\partial p_e^r}{\partial \tau} = \frac{r_a}{2}$ then $\frac{\partial \zeta}{\partial \tau} > 0$ and $\frac{\partial \hat{D}_e}{\partial \tau} > 0$, if

$$r_{AF} > \hat{r} = r_a \left(1 - \frac{1}{2}\frac{D_e - (1-\delta)K_{e_T}}{K_a^d}\right)$$

Vice versa, if $r_{AF} < \hat{r}$ then $\frac{\partial \hat{D}_e}{\partial \tau} < 0$.

From (4.17), since $\frac{\partial p_e^r}{\partial \tau} = \frac{r_{AF}}{2}$ then $\frac{\partial \zeta}{\partial \tau} > 0$ and $\frac{\partial \hat{D}_e}{\partial \tau} > 0$, if

$$r_a > \hat{r} = r_{AF} \left(1 - \frac{1}{2}\frac{D_e - (1-\delta)K_{e_T}}{K_g^d}\right)$$

Vice versa, if $r_a < \hat{r}$ then $\frac{\partial \hat{D}_e}{\partial \tau} < 0$.

In conclusion $\frac{\partial \hat{D}_e}{\partial \tau} > 0$ if

$$\bar{r} > \hat{r} = \underline{r} \left(1 - \frac{1}{2}\frac{D_e - (1-\delta)K_{e_T}}{K_g^d}\right)$$

When the natural gas market is fully competitive then $\bar{r} = r_g$ and $\underline{r} = r_a$ if $\tau < \tau^s$ while $\bar{r} = r_a$ and $\underline{r} = r_g$ if $\tau \geq \tau^s$. When the natural gas market is imperfectly competitive then $\bar{r} = r_{AF}$ and $\underline{r} = r_a$ if $\tau < \tau^s$ while $\bar{r} = r_a$ and $\underline{r} = r_{AF}$ if $\tau \geq \tau^s$.

It is to be noted that when $\tau \geq \tau^s$ then $\left(\frac{\partial \hat{D}_e}{\partial \tau}\right)_{\tau<\tau^s} > 0$ always. Then, since $\Delta \hat{D}_e$ can be expressed as

$$\Delta \hat{D}_e = \int_0^{\tau^s} \left(\frac{\partial \hat{D}_e}{\partial \tau}\right)_{\tau<\tau^s} d\tau + \int_{\tau^s}^{\tau} \left(\frac{\partial \hat{D}_e}{\partial \tau}\right)_{\tau\geq\tau^s} d\tau$$

For a given τ and a given τ^s, $\Delta \hat{D}_e > 0$ when $\left(\frac{\partial \hat{D}_e}{\partial \tau}\right)_{\tau<\tau^s} < 0$ and $\left|\frac{\partial \hat{D}_e}{\partial \tau}\right|_{\tau<\tau^s}$ is sufficiently high and/or $\left|\frac{\partial \hat{D}_e}{\partial \tau}\right|_{\tau\geq\tau^s}$ is sufficiently low. This can occur when the dominant firm holds a low share of gas units (high $\underline{\mu}^{d_e} = \mu_a^{d_e}$ when $\tau < \tau^s$; low $\underline{\mu}^{d_e} = \mu_g^{d_e}$ when $\tau \geq \tau^s$). Finally, note that $\left|\frac{\partial \hat{D}_e}{\partial \tau}\right|$ is an increasing function of τ.

Proof of Lemma 2bis

From (4.8) and (4.9)

$$D_e \geq \hat{D}_{e_1} = \left[\underline{\mu}^{d_e} \delta\, \sigma + (1-\delta)\right] K_{e_T} \tag{4.18}$$

and from (4.11) and (4.12)

$$D_e \geq \hat{D}_{e_2} = (1-\delta)\left[\frac{1-\sigma\underline{\mu}^{f_e}}{1-\sigma}\right] K_{e_T} \tag{4.19}$$

where $\sigma = \dfrac{\overline{MC}_e - \underline{MC}_e}{\hat{p}_e - \underline{MC}_e}$

Proof of Lemma 3bis

The derivative of $\hat{D}_e$ with respect to τ can be written as

$$\frac{\partial \hat{D}_e}{\partial \tau} = \frac{\partial \hat{D}_e}{\partial \sigma}\frac{\partial \sigma}{\partial \tau} \tag{4.20}$$

Since (from (4.18) and (4.19))

$$\frac{\partial \hat{D}_{e_1}}{\partial \sigma} = \underline{\mu}^{d_e} \cdot \delta \cdot K_{e_T} > 0 \tag{4.21a}$$

and

$$\frac{\partial \hat{D}_{e_2}}{\partial \sigma} = \frac{(1-\delta)(1-\underline{\mu}^{f_e})}{(1-\sigma)^2} K_{e_T} > 0 \tag{4.21b}$$

then the degree of market power is a decreasing function of σ.

By differentiating σ with respect to τ and given that $\hat{p}_e$ and that c_{e_g} depends on τ, we get

$$\frac{\partial \sigma}{\partial \tau} = \frac{1}{(\hat{p}_e - c_{e_a} - r_a \tau)^2} \left[(r_{AF} - r_a)(\hat{p}_e(0) - c_{e_a}) - (\partial \hat{p}_e / \partial \tau - r_a)(c_{e_g}(0) - c_{e_a}) \right] \tag{4.22}$$

if $\tau < \tau^s$.

and

$$\frac{\partial \sigma}{\partial \tau} = \frac{1}{(\hat{p}_e - c_{e_g} - r_g \tau)^2} \left[(r_a - r_{AF})(\hat{p}_e(0) - c_{e_g}(0)) - (\partial \hat{p}_e / \partial \tau - r_{AF})(c_{e_a} - c_{e_g}(0)) \right] \tag{4.23}$$

if $\tau \geq \tau^s$.

From (4.22)

$\frac{\partial \sigma}{\partial \tau} > 0$ and $\frac{\partial \hat{D}_e}{\partial \tau} > 0$, if $\partial \hat{p}_e / \partial \tau < \hat{r} = r_a + \lambda(r_{AF} - r_a)$

with $\lambda = (\hat{p}_e(0) - c_{e_a})/(c_{e_g}(0) - c_{e_a})$. Vice versa, if $\partial \hat{p}_e / \partial \tau > \hat{r}$ then $\frac{\partial \hat{D}_e}{\partial \tau} < 0$.

From (4.23)

$\frac{\partial \sigma}{\partial \tau} > 0$ and $\frac{\partial \hat{D}_e}{\partial \tau} > 0$, if $\partial \hat{p}_e / \partial \tau < \hat{r} = r_{AF} + \lambda(r_a - r_{AF})$ with $\lambda = (\hat{p}_e(0) - c_{e_g})/(c_{e_a}(0) - c_{e_g})$. Vice versa, if $\partial \hat{p}_e / \partial \tau > \hat{r}$ then $\frac{\partial \hat{D}_e}{\partial \tau} < 0$.

Proof of Corollary 3

The following procedure is based on the assumption that the dominant firm considers the profit in each hour of the year separately. In other words, the dominant firm looks at the target in each hour of the year regardless of what may happen in the remaining hours.

When $D_e \in \left]\bar{K}_e; \underline{K}_e^{f_e}\right]$ the profit that the dominant firm earns by setting the price threshold before the implementation of the ETS is

$$\hat{\pi}_e(0) = (\hat{p}_e(0) - c_{e_a})RD_e(\hat{p}_e(0)) \tag{4.24}$$

with $RD_e = D_e - K^{f_e}$.

After the ETS the profit is

$$\hat{\pi}_{e_1}(\tau) = (\hat{p}_{e_1}(\tau) - MC_{e_a})RD_e(\hat{p}_{e_1}(\tau)) + \tau \cdot r_{bn} \cdot \bar{q}^{d_e} \tag{4.25}$$

Then, $\hat{\pi}_{e_1}(\tau) = \hat{\pi}_e(0)$ implies that

$$\begin{aligned}(\hat{p}_{e_1}(\tau) - c_{e_a}) = (\hat{p}_{e_1}(0) - c_{e_a})\frac{RD_e(\hat{p}_e(0))}{RD_e(\hat{p}_{e_1}(\tau))} + \\ - \tau \cdot r_{bn} \cdot \frac{\bar{q}_e^{d_e}}{RD_e(\hat{p}_{e_1}(\tau))} + \tau \cdot r_a\end{aligned} \tag{4.26}$$

Under full auctioning ($r_{bn} = 0$), (4.26) implies that $(\hat{p}_e(\tau) - \hat{p}_e(0)) > r_a \cdot \tau$. Under benchmarking ($r_{bn} > 0$), then $(\hat{p}_{e_1}(\tau) - \hat{p}_e(0)) < r_a \cdot \tau$

If the profit target is a short-term one, under auctioning market power never decreases. In fact, in order to maintain the profit constant, the price threshold has to increase more than the increase in marginal cost of the more efficient (more polluting) plants ($\Delta\hat{p}_e > \Delta MC_a = r_a\tau$).

Finally it remains to analyze the case in which the dominant firm pursues a long-term profit target (e.g., multiperiod) with the limit to ensure some stability in prices. Consider three periods: the initial one, before the ETS ($\tau = 0$); the period $t = 1$, after the implementation of the ETS, in which the carbon price increases by τ and the subsequent period $t = 2$ in which the carbon price decreases by τ. The dominant firm aims at maintaining the average profit (over the two periods after the ETS) equal to the initial profit, $\hat{\pi}_{e_1} + \hat{\pi}_{e_1} = 2\hat{\pi}_e(0)$, at the same time reducing the price volatility.

If, in the first period, the dominant firm sets a price lower than the price corresponding to the profit invariance, $\hat{p}_1^* < \hat{p}_1$, the profit loss will be

$$\begin{aligned}\Delta\hat{\pi}_{e_1}(\tau) = \left[\hat{p}_{e_1}^* - (c_{e_a} + r_a\tau)\right]RD_e(\hat{p}_{e_1}^*) + \\ - [\hat{p}_e(0) - c_{e_a}]RD_e(\hat{p}_e(0)) < 0\end{aligned}$$

In order to keep constant the average profit, in the second period the dominant firm will choose a price, $\hat{p}_{e_2}^*$, such that

$$\left[\hat{p}^*_{e_2} - c_a\right] RD_e(\hat{p}^*_{e_2}) + \left[\hat{p}^*_{e_1}(\tau) - (c_{e_a} + r_a\tau)\right] RD_e(\hat{p}^*_{e_1}) = \\ = 2[\hat{p}_e(0) - c_a)] RD_e(\hat{p}_e(0)) - 2r_{bn}\ \tau\ \bar{q}_e^{d_e} \tag{4.27}$$

From (4.27), $\hat{p}^*_{e_2} < \hat{p}^*_{e_1}$ if

$$\left[\hat{p}^*_{e_1}(\tau) - c_{e_a}\right] > r_a \tau \frac{RD_e(\hat{p}^*_{e_1})}{RD_e(\hat{p}^*_{e_1}) + RD_e(\hat{p}^*_{e_2})} + \\ + 2[(\hat{p}_e(0) - c_{e_a}) - r_{bn}\tau] \frac{RD_e(\hat{p}_e(0))}{RD_e(\hat{p}^*_{e_1}) + RD_e(\hat{p}^*_{e_2})} \tag{4.28}$$

Now, by subtracting the expression $\hat{p}_e(0) - c_{e_a}$ from either the right side or the left side of (4.28), in infinitesimal terms we get

$$\left(\frac{\partial \hat{p}_e}{\partial \tau}\right)_{t=1} = \lim_{\tau \to 0} \frac{\left[\hat{p}^*_{e_1}(\tau) - \hat{p}_e(0)\right]}{\tau} > \frac{1}{2} r_a - r_{bn}$$

Therefore, since $\hat{p}_e(0) < \hat{p}^*_{e_2}(\tau) < \hat{p}^*_{e_1}(\tau)$, in infinitesimal terms if $\left(\frac{\partial \hat{p}_e}{\partial \tau}\right)_{t=1} > \frac{1}{2} r_a$ or $\left(\frac{\partial \hat{p}_e}{\partial \tau}\right)_{t=1} > \frac{1}{2} r_a - r_{bn}$, under auctioning and benchmarking, respectively, then $\left(\frac{\partial \hat{p}_e}{\partial \tau}\right)_{t=2} > -\left(\frac{\partial \hat{p}_e}{\partial \tau}\right)_{t=1}$.

If firms hold both kinds of plants, it is to be noted that when $D_e \in]D_{e_M}; \bar{K}_e]$ both kinds of dominant firm's plants are dispatched: kind a with capacity $K_a^{d_e}$; kind g with capacity $D_e - (K_a^{d_e} - K^{f_e})$. Therefore, the conditions above become:

$$\left(\frac{\partial \hat{p}_e}{\partial \tau}\right)_{t=1} > \frac{1}{2} r_m$$

or

$$\left(\frac{\partial \hat{p}_e}{\partial \tau}\right)_{t=1} > \frac{1}{2} r_m - r_{bn}$$

with

$$r_m = \frac{r_a K_a^{d_e} + r_g\left[D_e - (K_a^{d_e} + K^{f_e})\right]}{K_a^{d_e} + \left[D_e - (K_a^{d_e} + K^{f_e})\right]}$$

Obviously when the dominant firm holds only plants a then $r_m = r_a$.

Proof of Corollary 4

When the dominant firm pursues a short-term target, since $\frac{\partial \hat{p}_e}{\partial \tau} > r_a$, the condition for decreasing market power (see Lemma 3bis), $\frac{\partial \hat{p}_e}{\partial \tau} < \hat{r} = r_a + \lambda(r_{AF} - r_a)$, becomes

$$r_{AF} > \hat{r} = r_a \left[1 + (\rho - 1)\frac{D_e - K^f}{K_a^d}\right]$$

with $\rho > 1$, under taxation or ETS with auctioning.

Conversely, with ETS and benchmarking, the change in the price cap is net of the carbon cost of the benchmark technology, $\frac{\partial \hat{p}_e}{\partial \tau} > r_a - r_{bn}$. As a consequence the condition for decreasing market power is

$$r_{AF} > \hat{r} = r_a \left[1 + (\rho - 1)\frac{D_e - K^f}{K_a^d}\right] - \rho\, r_{bn}\frac{D_e - K^f}{K_a^d}$$

Proof of Corollary 5

When the dominant firm pursues a long-term target then $\frac{\partial \hat{p}_e}{\partial \tau} > \frac{1}{2} r_a$. In this case the condition for decreasing market power, $\frac{\partial \hat{p}_e}{\partial \tau} < \hat{r} = r_a + \lambda(r_{AF} - r_a)$, becomes

$$r_{AF} > \hat{r} = r_a \left[1 + \left(\frac{\rho}{2} - 1\right)\frac{D_e - K^f}{K_a^d}\right]$$

with ETS and auctioning.

If allowances are benchmarked then $\frac{\partial \hat{p}_e}{\partial \tau} > \frac{1}{2} r_a - r_{bn}$. The condition for decreasing market power becomes:

$$r_{AF} > \hat{r} = r_a \left[1 + \left(\frac{\rho}{2} - 1\right)\frac{D_e - K^f}{K_a^d}\right] - \rho\, r_{bn}\frac{D_e - K^f}{K_a^d}$$

Proof of Equation (4.5)

Given the load duration curves in Figs. 4.4 and 4.5, the total amount of pollutant emissions, E, under imperfect competition is

$$E_{ic} = r_g\left[\int_0^{\hat{H}} D_e(H,\hat{p}_e)dH\right] + r_g\left[\int_{\hat{H}}^{\underline{H}} D_e(H,\hat{p}_e)dH\right] + (r_g - r_a)(K_{e_T}\hat{H} - K^{d_e}\underline{H}) + \\ + r_a\left[\int_{-H(\tau)}^{H_L(\tau)} D_e(H,\hat{p}_e)dH\right]$$

And under full competition

$$E_{fc} = r_g\int_0^{\underline{H}} D_e dH + r_a\left[\int_{\underline{H}}^{H_L} D_e dH\right]$$

By differentiating E_{ic} and E_{fc} with respect to τ and given that

$$\frac{\partial}{\partial\tau}\left[\int_{H_i(p_e(\tau))}^{H_j(p_e(\tau))} D_e(H,p_e(\tau))dH\right] = D_e(H_j,p_e(\tau))\frac{\partial H_j}{\partial\tau} - D_e(H_i,p(\tau))\frac{\partial H_i}{\partial\tau} + \\ + \int_{H_i(p_e(\tau))}^{H_j(p_e(\tau))} \frac{\partial D_e(H,p(\tau))}{\partial\tau}dH$$

and that $\beta = -\frac{\partial D_e}{\partial p_e} = -\frac{\partial D_e}{\partial\tau}\Big/\frac{\partial p_e}{\partial\tau}$ we get

$$\frac{\partial E_{ic}}{\partial\tau} = r_a\left[-\beta\frac{\partial\hat{p}_e}{\partial\tau}\int_0^{\hat{H}} D_e dH\right] + (r_g - r_a)\left[(K_{e_T} - \hat{D}_e)\frac{\partial\hat{H}}{\partial\tau}\right] + \\ + r_g\left[-\beta\, r_{AF}\int_{\hat{H}}^{\underline{H}} D_e dH\right] + r_a\left[-\beta\, r_{AF}\int_{\underline{H}}^{H_L} D_e dH\right] \tag{4.29}$$

and

$$\frac{\partial E_{fc}}{\partial\tau} = r_g\left[-\beta\, r_g\int_0^{\underline{H}} D_e dH\right] + r_a\left[-\beta\, r_a\int_{\underline{H}}^{H_L} D_e dH\right] \tag{4.30}$$

Where $\frac{\partial \hat{H}}{\partial \tau}$ includes two components: $\frac{\partial H}{\partial D_e}\frac{\partial \hat{D}_e}{\partial \tau}$ which is the change in $\hat{H}$ due to the change in $\hat{D}_e$ (see Lemma 3 and Lemma 3bis); $\frac{\partial H}{\partial D_e}\frac{\partial D_e}{\partial p_e}\frac{\partial p_e}{\partial \tau} = -\beta\frac{\partial H}{\partial D_e}\frac{\partial p_e}{\partial \tau}$ which is the change in $\hat{H}$ to the change in demand.

By replacing these components in (4.29) and by subtracting $\frac{\partial E_{fc}}{\partial \tau}$ from $\frac{\partial E_{ic}}{\partial \tau}$ we get the difference in marginal emissions between imperfect and full competition [(4.5) in Section 5].

References

Canton J, Saubeyran A, Stahn H (2008) Environmental taxation and vertical Cournot oligopolies: how eco-industries matter. Environ Resour Econ 40:369–382

Chernyavs'ka L, Gullì F (2008a) Marginal CO_2 cost pass-through under imperfect competition. Ecol Econ 68:408–421

Chernyavs'ka L, Gullì F (2008b) The impact of the European Emissions Trading Scheme on power prices in Italy: the "load duration curve approach". In: Gullì F (ed) Markets for carbon and power pricing in Europe: theoretical issues and empirical analyses. Edward Elgar, Aldershot, UK, and Brookfield, WI

Conrad K, Wang J (1993) The effect of emission taxes and abatement subsides on market structure. Int J Ind Organ 11:499–518

Denny E, O'Malley M (2009) The impact of carbon prices on generation-cycling costs. Energy Policy 37:1204–1212

Fabra N, von der Fehr N, Harbord D (2002) Modeling electricity auctions. Electr J 15(7)

Garcia-Diaz A, Marin L (2003) Strategic bidding in electricity pools with short-lived bids: an application to the Spanish market. Int J Ind Organ 21:201–222

Gullì F (2008) Modeling the short-run impact of carbon emissions trading on the electricity sector. In: Gullì F (ed) Markets for carbon and power pricing in Europe: theoretical issues and empirical analyses. Edward Elgar, Aldershot, UK, and Brookfield, WI

Levin D (1985) Taxation within Cournot oligopoly. J Public Econ 27:281–290

Requate T (2005) Environmental policy under imperfect competition – a survey. CAU, Economics Working Papers, 2005–12

Sijm S, Hers S, Wetzelaer B (2008a) Options to address concerns regarding EU ETS-induced increases in power prices and generators' profits: the case of carbon cost pass-through in Germany and the Netherlands. In: Gullì F (ed) Markets for carbon and power pricing in Europe: theoretical issues and empirical analyses. Edward Elgar, Aldershot, UK and Brookfield, WI

Sijm J, Hers S, Lise W, Wetzelaer B (2008b) The impact of the EU ETS on electricity prices. Final report to the European Commission (DG Environment), Energy research Centre of the Netherlands, ECN-E-08-007, Petten/Amsterdam

Sugeta H, Matsumoto S (2007) Upstream and downstream pollution taxations in vertically related markets with imperfect competition. Environ Resour Econ 38:407–432

Vivid Economics (2007) A study to estimate ticket price changes for aviation in the EU ETS. A Report to DEFRA and DfT, London, UK

von der Fehr N, Harbord D (1993) Spot market competition in the UK electricity industry. Econ J 103(418):531–546

von der Fehr N, Harbord D (1998) Competition in electricity spot markets – economic theory and international experience. Memorandum, n. 5, Department of Economics, University of Oslo

Lightning Source UK Ltd.
Milton Keynes UK
UKOW030011230113

205211UK00002B/149/P

9 781447 147268